CW00669616

The Healthy Company

by

Mervyn King

and

Leigh Roberts

juta

The Healthy Company

First published 2021

© Juta and Company (Pty) Ltd
First Floor, Sunclare Building, 21 Dreyer Street,
Claremont, 7708, Cape Town
www.juta.co.za

This book is copyright under the Berne Convention. In terms of the Copyright Act, No 98 of 1978, no part of this book may be reproduced or transmitted in any form or by any means, electronic or mechanical, including photocopying, recording or by any information storage and retrieval system, without permission in writing from the publisher.

The authors and the publisher believe on the strength of due diligence exercised that this work does not contain any material that is the subject of copyright held by another person. In the alternative, they believe that any protected pre-existing material that may be comprised in it has been used with appropriate authority or has been used in such circumstances that make such use permissible under the law.

Although every care is taken to ensure the accuracy of this publication, supplements, updates and replacement material, the authors, editors, publishers and printers do not accept responsibility for any act, omission, loss, damage or the consequences thereof occasioned by a reliance by any person upon the contents hereof.

ISBN: 978 1 48513 746 7

Project specialist: Samantha Simmons
Editor: Linda van de Vijver
Cover Design: Renaissance Studio
Typesetter: Warda Essa

juta

CONTENTS

About the Authors

Mervyn E King SC

Mervyn King is an internationally known corporate lawyer and a professor on corporate governance who has chaired companies listed on the London, Luxembourg and Johannesburg stock exchanges. He has chaired the United Nations Committee of Eminent Persons on Governance and Oversight and is Chairman Emeritus of the International Integrated Reporting Council and the GRI, and of the King Committee which produced the King Codes of Governance. Mervyn has consulted, advised and spoken on legal, business, advertising, sustainability and governance issues in over 60 countries. He is a Senior Counsel and former Judge of the Supreme Court of South Africa.

Leigh Roberts

Leigh Roberts has been deeply involved in integrated reporting in South Africa and internationally since its emergence in 2010. She worked on the development of the International <IR> Framework released in 2013 and its revision in 2021. She has consulted and run board and executive training on integrated reporting internationally and in South Africa and has written numerous publications. Leigh is the Chief Executive Officer of the Integrated Reporting Committee of South Africa and is its technical head. She has adjudicated for integrated reporting awards, is a Chartered Accountant and an award-winning business journalist in print and television.

Foreword

'The role of thinkers ... is primarily to have available alternatives, so when the brute force of events make a change inevitable, there is an alternative available to change it.'

Milton Friedman *Money Programme Transcripts* (1978)

When Milton Friedman made this declaration over the airwaves of the BBC in 1978, the global capital markets were on the precipice of a fundamental shift towards an era of shareholder primacy. Although this wave of change might have felt like a decisive and abrupt market force, Friedman's point was that the intellectual groundwork had been laid over the previous three decades. Friedman's famous assertion that 'there is one and only one social responsibility of business – to use its resources and engage in activities designed to increase its profits' actually first appeared in his 1962 book *Capitalism and Freedom*. The intellectual movement can be traced further back to Friedrich Hayek's gathering of the Mont Pelerin Society in 1947. Fundamental market shifts do not necessarily happen in conjunction with the development of new tools and theories; rather, new tools and theories are adopted when the status quo becomes untenable.

Today, we find ourselves at one of those inflection points because we have arrived at a pivotal moment for the future of capitalism. On the heels of the 2008 global financial crisis, we have seen a growing mistrust of the financial industry and business communities. Even as economies and stock markets have rebounded, the gains were largely enjoyed by those at the top. The marked and accelerating income inequality has led many to feel that capitalism is simply not working for them. This widespread sense of alienation and isolation has contributed to growing populist movements around the globe and an erosion of the public's trust in the private sector. In this case, the 'brute force of events' that has made change inevitable, somewhat ironically, is Milton Friedman's shareholder primacy approach to capitalism.

The reality is that systems like capitalism should and must evolve as the societies in which they operate evolve. Our economic system is undergoing a period of transformation that has been unmatched in the last hundred years. When the teachings of Milton Friedman were gaining traction in the 1970s, more than 80 per cent of a company's market capitalisation was represented by tangible assets that could be found on its balance sheet. Today, tangible assets represent less than 15 per cent of a company's market capitalisation on average in the S&P 500.[1] Management, boards and investors cannot simply rely on financial statements to tell the whole story of future value.

Mervyn King has spent the better part of two decades championing the movement to better understand and develop frameworks for integrated reporting that capture the interconnected nature of a company's financial performance and performance around sustainability issues. If companies think about human capital, stakeholder relationships and financial performance holistically, why should the reporting of financials and sustainability be siloed instead of reflective of that interconnectedness? Through his leadership at the United Nations, the Global Reporting Initiative and the International Integrated Reporting Council (in partnership with HRH Prince Charles' Accounting for Sustainability), King has led a heroic effort to lay the groundwork for this market transformation and deserves a tremendous amount of credit for the USD$30 trillion currently invested in ESG strategies globally.[2]

While substantial progress has been made, macro trends are necessitating a structural, systemic change among business, investors and policy makers. A passive reliance on the status quo will be insufficient to mitigate the risks and to capitalise on the opportunities of the changing economic landscape. At the 2014 Conference on Inclusive Capitalism, Governor Mark Carney said 'unchecked market fundamentalism can devour the social capital essential for the long-term dynamism of capitalism itself.' Instead, a variety of stakeholders, from companies to the capital markets to policy makers, must act with a sense of shared responsibility for the broader system – not at the expense of their own self-interest, but because acting with a sense of purpose and responsibility towards the wider system will provide better outcomes for the individual, the investor, the company and society over the long term. *The Healthy Company* helps to identify how corporations, investors and business leaders can establish the right mindset and use the right tools to re-orient markets towards long-term success and to promote broadly shared prosperity.

This represents a shift from the shareholder primacy model of capitalism that has been prevalent over the last half century. But, in reality, it just represents

---

[1] Annual Study of Intangible Asset Market Value from Ocean Tomo, LLC at https://www.oceantomo.com/2015/03/04/2015-intangible-asset-market-value-study/.

[2] Global Sustainable Investment Alliance, '2018 Global Sustainable Investment Review' at http://www.gsi-alliance.org/wp-content/uploads/2019/03/GSIR_Review2018.3.28.pdf.

a return to the original intention of capitalism and market-based economies. Companies exist for the purpose of providing goods and services and solving problems in society. Collectively, companies, investors and policy makers must foster a more inclusive form of capitalism in order to keep their licence to operate. To survive, capitalism must become more inclusive, sustainable, dynamic and trusted. Inclusive capitalism can only be achieved by properly understanding, incentivising and measuring the actions that create sustainable value over the long term. But this will be a journey. Catalysing such a tremendous undertaking requires a deep understanding of how we ended up in this situation and a specific vision of how to achieve a better future.

In *The Healthy Company*, Mervyn King and Leigh Roberts brilliantly and succinctly contextualise the evolution of our economic system that led to shareholder primacy, articulate the structural shifts in society that have placed tensions on that philosophy, and provide a roadmap to achieve a healthier and more prosperous future for all stakeholders. Their work is informative but not prescriptive; it does not serve as a checklist of actions. Instead, this book will challenge business leaders to take a deep and holistic look at their company and its resources, both internal and external, to form a holistic view of how they interact with and influence the activities that create financial, societal and environmental value.

Lynn Forester de Rothschild

October 2020

Foreword

It is common knowledge that the 2008 global financial crisis made it glaringly obvious that the level and quality of financial disclosure (not to mention non-financial disclosure) and the aggregation of risk exposure of some of the biggest financial institutions in the world, generally, were hopelessly insufficient and inadequate. This gave rise to the concepts of integrated reporting and integrated thinking.

When the subject of integrated reporting was first raised and explained to me around this time by the highly intelligent (and charming) Leigh Roberts, I knew the Johannesburg Stock Exchange (JSE), of which I was the CEO at the time, had to get involved at an early stage. And we did.

My contention at the time was that integrated reporting and integrated thinking were not completely new concepts; rather, it was a case of many companies not always telling stakeholders what they were doing and what they were thinking. A case in point is the Central Securities Depository of South Africa, Strate (Pty) Limited. This little known and little understood company fulfils an absolutely critical role in the daily functioning of South Africa's financial markets. An analysis of its Annual Financial Statements (AFS) before the integrated reporting age would have left one none the wiser as to the role of this company. Nowadays, the integrated reports of Strate provide one with a very good idea of its role and function in society, even if one is not financially literate.

The preparation of the AFS and the reports issued by a company are the responsibility of the board of directors, and chapters 2 and 3 of *The Healthy Company* make poignant points on new ways for a company to think about the reason to exist.

This book should be prescribed as compulsory reading for those in private sector companies, as well as for bureaucrats, politicians and governments. Integrated thinking needs to be impregnated into the often pitiful, corruption-prone minds of many politicians – for the governance of a country should be subject to the same amount of scrutiny as the governance of a company. Politicians should be as accountable as boards of directors. Politicians nowadays, the world over, often seem to be oblivious or impervious to the effects their decisions have on the environment or the economy, or, finally, on society itself.

I like the way in which this book weaves the first, second, third and fourth industrial revolutions, as well as the original creation of the artificial legal person being the limited liability company, into the functioning of a board of directors. I would add that anybody who accepts a non-executive position at a private sector company (or a state-owned company, particularly in the case of South Africa), without a very good working knowledge of the broad operating model (financial as well as non-financial aspects) of the company and who does not know and trust the management and fellow board members totally, needs to reflect, seriously.

Chapter 10 correctly makes the point that the integrated report can be likened to the tip of the iceberg whereas integrated thinking is the body of the iceberg. In our connected world of the 21st century, integrated thinking is the only way of leading and managing a company. This chapter also provides good guidance for the board and management regarding the preparation of the annual integrated report.

South Africa has been very fortunate to have the likes of Mervyn King (Mr. Corporate Governance) and Leigh Roberts lead the way with King I, King II, King III and King IV (stretching over more than two decades) and integrated reporting. They founded the Integrated Reporting Committee (IRC) of South Africa in 2010 and their ongoing leadership has ensured that South Africa continues to be regarded as the home of integrated reporting. They have done South Africa proud. We owe them!

The Healthy Company is a very practical guide on the management, governance and reporting of a modern-day 21st century company. I highly recommend it.

Russell Loubser

Non-executive director of companies

October 2020

Chapter 1   Coronanomics

Corporate leaders no longer make decisions in the best interests of creating wealth for shareholders. Today, leaders make decisions in the best interests of the long-term health of the company. This is the art of doing business in the 21ˢᵗ century.

In making informed decisions for the long-term health of the company, corporate leaders have to know and understand the legitimate and reasonable needs, interests, expectations and troubles of the company's stakeholders.

Amongst many new agenda items for a company's board of directors, stakeholder relationships should be a standing item. Arise the corporate stakeholder relationship officer, whose sole job is to learn about the continuing relationship between the company and its stakeholders and present a written report at each board meeting. Up-to-date knowledge gives the board more informed oversight. It gives the company's management a more informed basis for strategy, risks and opportunities, and healthy decision-making.

This informed oversight can better enable corporate leaders to lead the company through the Great Reset of the 2020s – the coronavirus pandemic. Two crises – economic and viral – are twisting together in a sea of coronanomics. Companies big and small are swimming in this sea and, in the short term, the board has to ensure that the company stays afloat.

The Sustainable Development Goals (SDGs), issued by the United Nations in 2015 and embraced by 193 countries, encompass the three dimensions for the long-term health of a company: the environment, the economy and society (EES). The three are inherently interconnected and should be thought of in an integrated way.

In capital raising nowadays, investment institutions not only undertake financial due diligence but also environmental, social and governance (ESG) due diligence in the acknowledgement that they are essential to the company's health. Furthermore, many countries have issued prudential investment guidelines. In South Africa, the Financial Services Conduct Authority has guidelines on how the trustees of pension funds and directors of financial institutions need to take account of ESG factors before investing the beneficiaries' money in the equity of a company.

The relevance in the sea of coronanomics is that corporate leaders have to approach doing business in an integrated fashion. They have to know the needs, interests, expectations, hardships and tribulations of the company's stakeholders, as well as the resource constraints, and apply integrated thinking. This is a time for collaboration – which also happens to be the focus of SDG 17.

In the short term, the mindset of corporate leaders in the Great Reset of the early 2020s has to be integrated, collaborative, compassionate and compromising. Compromises by a company with and by its stakeholders may be the only way for the company – even on a reduced basis – to stay afloat in the coronavirus sea.

If companies can survive the short term, they also position the economy for a quicker bounce to growth recovery. For if these companies are liquidated now, the infrastructure disappears, the human resources are dispersed, the culture created by the company is gone, and its assets are probably sold at knock-down auction prices. To recreate the business of these companies will result in a much slower economic recovery. It will be easier and faster to resurrect a company that stayed afloat in a reduced form, than to liquidate the company and then endeavour to start a new company and a new business.

In short, boards must have a company-centric and informed stakeholder approach in making judgement calls for the survival of the company. In turn, stakeholders will find that they also need an approach of compromise in the sea of coronanomics. For example, management and staff may need to take a pay cut, suppliers may need to reduce the cost of goods in the supply chain, and banks may need to give payment holidays or reduced rates of interest. These are some of the compromises made between stakeholders and companies.

Whilst this mindset change is necessary now, other clouds are gaining momentum. These are the clouds of climate change. Boards cannot ignore the impact of climate change on the company's business model and its strategic direction. It is a crucial factor in the long-term health of the company, and requires ensuring that the company takes account of a 2 to 3 degrees Celsius increase in temperature in the near term – with all the consequences, such as rising sea water, drought, increased poverty, migration, etc – and avoids or mitigates its own carbon emissions in the shift to renewable energy and the green economy.

Whilst humanity has been able to self-isolate, socially distance, wash hands and wear masks during the coronavirus pandemic, none of these measures can help with a significant jump in temperature. The healthy company is one where the board, whilst having this collaborative, compromising mindset for near-term survival, must continue to plan for the impact that climate change will have on the company's business model and its long-term health.

The Healthy Company can help boards around the world think in an integrated way and thereby help to ensure the long-term health of their companies, which is in the long-term better interests of the company's stakeholders.

Chapter 2 The Now Way

The 19th and 20th centuries will go down in history as the era of unsustainable development. This was the result of some fundamental wrongs committed in the prevailing corporate doctrines:

Acting in the best interests of shareholders: Since the advent of the legal structure of the company in the 19th century, directors have focused on creating shareholder gains via earnings, free cash flow, dividends and share price. The remuneration of executive directors depended upon this, based on the venerated corporate tenet of aligning the directors' interests with those of shareholders.

A misguided duty of care: Directors have an inherent duty of care – but this was erroneously guided to the shareholders. As the stewards of the company their legal duty is making decisions or acting in the best interests of the company for the long term.

Definition of success: The focus on shareholder gains prompted the narrow view of success as solely financial: ever-rising earnings, effective cost management, strong cash flow, higher dividends, a growth strategy and a resilient share price. This pursuit of financial performance had hidden – and sometimes not-so-hidden – costs which were borne by society and the environment. These were costs such as climate change, the shrinking supply of fresh water, the loss of forests and biodiversity, ocean pollution, land pollution and more. Strangely, directors were acting lawfully in their pursuit of profit, but they had caused their innocent charge, the company, to commit wrongs against society and the environment. It was a case of lawful wrongs.

Today, society is demanding that companies have sustainable value creation processes. These processes must be based on integrated thinking tailored for the 21st century with its technological advances, natural resource constraints, adversity to waste and increasing population. It's a progression – an evolution – in the mindset of doing business.

This move respects financial capital as well as other forms of capital. This move also recognises that looking at a company from only a financial perspective is akin to seeing only a single slice of the cake.

This progression acknowledges that resources and stakeholder relationships are what make a company tick – and continue ticking. There is evidence of this truism in the headlines of corporate scandals and drama of the 2010s. Invariably these scandals centred on the company's resources and relationships and the effects thereon of the company's business model, strategy and decisions. Environmental disasters, poor ethics, insufficient engagement with stakeholders on a new mine, the pressure of ever-rising sales targets, slack internal controls, non-compliance with regulations or poor corporate governance – all caused financial stress and reputational damage to the company. The resources the company depends on and the stakeholders it relies on can pose a real risk to the company because of their core nature to the business. But they can also pose opportunities.

The consideration of resources and stakeholder relationships is undeniably a part of the duty of care that directors have to the company. Directors cannot contend that they aren't aware of the changed world in which the company operates. They need to continually ask themselves: What do I know or what ought I to know? What am I aware of or what ought I to be aware of? A director may well be called upon to voice their answer in court when explaining their business judgement calls. The director's duty of care is more complex than ever.

A word on the trending use of the term 'stakeholder capitalism': It has become popular in some countries for directors to see their duty as stakeholder capitalism, that is, acting in the interests of all stakeholder groups. But this is merely a swopping out of errors from the interests of shareholders in the 20th century to the interests of stakeholders in the 21st century. Their common error is that they both ignore the directors' duty to the company itself – to focus on doing what is best for the company in the short, medium and long term. In doing what's best for the company there will always be trade-offs between the interests of various stakeholder groups, but the directors' actions will always be focused on looking after their charge, the company, after having considered the needs, interests and expectations of all stakeholders and not only shareholders. This duty to the company is almost a universal legal principle around the world.

And a word on shared value: this is based on stakeholder capitalism, but the problem is that it usually excludes any negative effects that the company and its products might be having on the environment, as well as any unintended outcomes on stakeholder groups. Moreover, it is a short-term view: for what is the good of positive outcomes on stakeholders at the expense of negative outcomes on the natural environment, since all are integrated in the long term?

The board would be wise to remember that the total assets of the company belong to the company and not to any stakeholder. The only way a shareholder can benefit is from a dividend which is declared by the board and paid if there is adequate liquidity. And a stakeholder can only benefit from delivering services and supplies to the company, with the environment sadly often used as a 'free' supplier.

A healthy board is essential for a healthy company.

Chapter 3   The Now Business Model

The companies that enjoy good long-term health in the 21ˢᵗ century will be those with boards who know that corporate dictates have evolved.

The board knows that:

- The company relies on a myriad of resources and stakeholder relationships and that understanding and nurturing them is the best path to long-term health.

- Its responsibility is to define the company's success as financial returns plus positive effects on society, the economy and the environment.

- The purpose of the company must embrace creating positive value for society, the economy and the environment.

- The parameters of the business model, strategy and business judgement calls are maximising the positive effects and avoiding or ameliorating the adverse ones on society, the economy and the environment.

- Society, with its power of radical transparency through social media, no longer accepts adverse effects on society, the economy and the environment.

- Ethics, values, culture and conduct are the life blood of the company and set the conscious, ethical behaviour of directors, executives and staff.

- Millennials and generation Z take an active interest in how the products they buy are made and the good corporate citizen status of the company behind them.

- Investors, especially larger institutions, regard companies that see social, economic and environmental matters as core to their business as probably having good quality conscious leadership and thus a greater chance of being around in the longer term.

- Society, the effective licensor of companies, wants directors to carry out their duties to the company for the betterment of society, the economy and the environment.

- The high contrast of the past shows that there is opportunity for change. It's a mindset shift.

The board knows this – and that there's academic research to back it up.

Harvard Business School has shown that:

- Sustainable companies deliver significant positive financial performance and investors are beginning to value them more highly.[3]

The University of Oxford and Arabesque Partners reviewed over 200 academic studies, industry reports, newspaper articles and books, and found that:

- 90 per cent of the studies on the cost of capital show that sound sustainability standards lower the cost of capital.

- 88 per cent of the research shows that solid environmental, social and governance practices result in better operational performance.

- 80 per cent of the studies show that the stock price performance of companies is positively influenced by good sustainability practices.[4]

In short, sustainability is good business sense.

The now business model

The now business model offers a holistic and long-term view of the company. It is an important awareness tool as it shows the company's dependency on and the effects it is having on its resources and stakeholder relationships, with financial performance being only one of the positive outcomes.

The now business model begins with the inputs drawn from resources and stakeholder relationships. They churn through the company's activities and operations to become its products, services and waste. These, in turn, have consequential effects on the input resources and stakeholder relationships to be used by the company in the future. It is a circle of connectivity, a circle of cause and effect.

The now business model is different from the 20th century traditional definition of the business model with its focus on revenue streams, markets and customers

[3] Robert G Eccles, Ioannis Ioannou & George Serafeim 'The impact of corporate sustainability on organizational processes and performance' (2014) 60(11) *Management Science* 2835.

[4] Gordon L Clark, Andreas Feiner & Michael Viehs *From the Stockholder to the Stakeholder: How Sustainability Can Drive Financial Outperformance* (March 2015), at https://arabesque.com/research/From_the_stockholder_to_the_stakeholder_web.pdf.

(being yesterday's definition of success). The problem with that model is that it stopped at products and services (and sometimes included waste) and didn't look further into the resulting effects on society, the economy and the environment which could impact the company's future. In other words, its singular financial focus was narrow and focused on a single slice of the cake.

Over the past decade there has been rising global acceptance of viewing resources and stakeholder relationships as different types of capital – six, to be exact, with financial capital being one of them. The six capitals idea first appeared in the *International <IR> Framework* released by the International Integrated Reporting Council in December 2013[5] and subsequently appeared in corporate governance codes such as the *King IV Report on Corporate Governance for South Africa 2016™*.[6] The advantage of seeing resources and stakeholder relationships as six capitals is that it triggers a mindset shift within the company and elevates awareness and respect for all the contributors to the company's success. Also, it is a useful completeness check to ensure that all inputs and effects are included in the business model and strategy. Figure 1 shows the six categories of capital outlined in the *International <IR> Framework*.

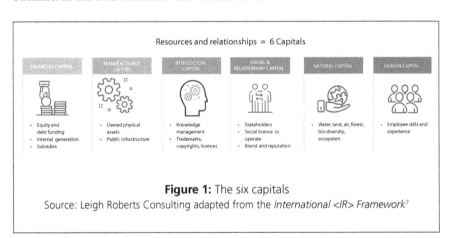

Figure 1: The six capitals
Source: Leigh Roberts Consulting adapted from the *International <IR> Framework*[7]

---

[5] The *International <IR> Framework* is available at www.integratedreporting.org.

[6] Copyrights and trademarks are owned by the Institute of Directors in Southern Africa NPC and all its rights are reserved. An online version of King IV is available at www.iodsa.co.za.

[7] This figure is based on International Integrated Reporting Council (IIRC) *International <IR> Framework (2021)* page 19.

Each capital can be regarded as a 'pool' or 'store of value' available for use, whether owned by the company or not. Inputs are drawn from the six capitals and the company in turn has effects (called outcomes) on the six capitals.

All if not most of the six capitals will be relevant to a company because it is not as simple as the extent of use or effect. Take the story of companies in Cape Town, South Africa. The drought of 2017/2018 prompted the stark realisation of 'no water, no business'. The severe usage restrictions imposed by the city's municipality as the dams dried up saw companies scrambling for new sources and new ways to recycle water for their hotels, offices, factories and shops.

The Cape Town story highlights that even if a company says natural capital is not material to it because of low usage and the nature of its business, natural capital is in fact material: no water, no business, no financial returns to shareholders, no positive outcomes for other stakeholders, no future for the company. The Cape Town story highlights the interdependence of and connections between the six capitals.

The coronavirus pandemic similarly shows this interdependence. The health of the people affected the health of the companies and the health of the economy.

Figure 2 depicts the business model with the flow of the six capitals from inputs to outcomes. The green arrows show the cause and effect loop where today's effects on the six capitals feed into tomorrow's inputs through aspects such as price, availability and quality.

Drawing up the company's business model will be worth the time spent. It is extremely useful in understanding all the company's inputs and outcomes. This awareness ensures that what matters gets into the company's measuring, monitoring and reporting systems. It can result in more informed decision-making through the availability of holistic information. The business model ensures that the company is better prepared.

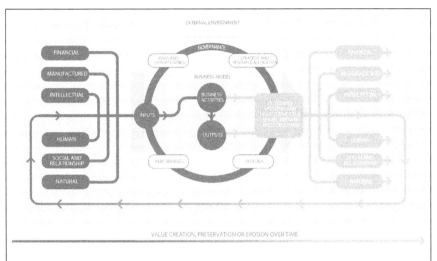

Figure 2: The process through which value is created, eroded or preserved[8]

---

[8] IIRC, *International <IR> Framework* (2021). This is reproduced with the IIRC's kind permission. This diagram is an update of the original version in IIRC *International <IR> Framework* (December 2013), and should be regarded as incomplete, with the final version appearing in the updated *International <IR> Framework*, due out in December 2020.

Chapter 4   Purpose, Outcomes and Strategy

The company's purpose

The now business model is positioned within the 'bubble' of the company's purpose. In the 20th century many directors set the company's purpose as maximising profit and shareholder wealth. In the 21st century there is recognition that the company's purpose encompasses both profit and positive outcomes on society, the economy and the environment.

It makes sense: Companies create goods and services to sell to people. People are the society. Why would society tolerate companies that harm people and the natural environment they live in and depend on? Society now has the power to object through the radical transparency afforded by the internet and social media.

Company purpose catapulted in topicality when Larry Fink, the chairman and CEO of BlackRock Inc, one of the world's biggest investors, wrote about it in his 2018 Letter to CEOs and then repeated the call in his 2019 Letter.

> We also see many governments failing to prepare for the future, on issues ranging from retirement and infrastructure to automation and worker retraining. As a result, society increasingly is turning to the private sector and asking that companies respond to broader societal challenges. Indeed, the public expectations of your company have never been greater. Society is demanding that companies, both public and private, serve a social purpose. To prosper over time, every company must not only deliver financial performance, but also show how it makes a positive contribution to society. Companies must benefit all of their stakeholders, including shareholders, employees, customers, and the communities in which they operate.

> Without a sense of purpose, no company, either public or private, can achieve its full potential. It will ultimately lose the license to operate from key stakeholders. It will succumb to short-term pressures to distribute earnings, and, in the process, sacrifice investments in employee development, innovation, and capital expenditures that are necessary

for long-term growth. It will remain exposed to activist campaigns that articulate a clearer goal, even if that goal serves only the shortest and narrowest of objectives.[9]

Profits are in no way inconsistent with purpose – in fact, profits and purpose are inextricably linked. Profits are essential if a company is to effectively serve all of its stakeholders over time – not only shareholders, but also employees, customers, and communities. Similarly, when a company truly understands and expresses its purpose, it functions with the focus and strategic discipline that drive long-term profitability. Purpose unifies management, employees, and communities. It drives ethical behavior and creates an essential check on actions that go against the best interests of stakeholders. Purpose guides culture, provides a framework for consistent decision-making, and, ultimately, helps sustain long-term financial returns for the shareholders of your company.[10]

It's obvious why BlackRock, with its trillions of dollars of assets under management, understands the worth of encouraging companies to deliver financial performance and a positive contribution to society, the economy and the environment. Much of BlackRock's investment money comes from investors saving for their retirement or other long-term savings goal – they really need the companies they invest in to render sustainable growth and to be around in the long term.

This highlights another 'perfect sense' circle: people entrust their savings to professional investors who invest in the very companies that the people work for or buy from. Why would they (as society) put up with companies that harm them and the natural environment in which they live and rely on?

The purpose of a company recognises the changed world in which we live and improves on the high contrast of the past.

[9] Larry Fink, BlackRock Inc 'Larry Fink's 2018 Letter to CEOs: A sense of purpose' at
     https://www.blackrock.com/corporate/investor-relations/2018-larry-fink-ceo-letter.
[10] Larry Fink, BlackRock Inc 'Larry Fink's 2019 Letter to CEOs: Purpose & Profit' at
     https://www.blackrock.com/corporate/investor-relations/2019-larry-fink-ceo-letter.

Outcomes

The outcomes of the company's activities and its products, services and waste – ie the effects on the six capitals (akin to impacts on society, economy and the environment) – can be positive, adverse or neutral. Outcomes can manifest immediately or appear over the short, medium or long term.

Some examples:

- A private schools company describes its positive effects on society as the quality of education that it provides and its contribution to the economy. On natural capital it describes how it minimises the direct adverse effects and that its positive effects include environmental awareness and projects in its schools' curricula.

- A bank that targets the lower-income market talks about the positive effects that its low-fee banking is having on the economy, and the positive effects on communities of increased access to banking facilities through its mobile banking vehicles. It also describes the negative effects of lending in this market (high debt levels of consumers and the inability to repay) with details of how it is working to minimise these adverse effects.

- A mining company's outcomes include its adverse effects on the environment and its mitigation plans, but also the positive effects of how the metal is used in society, the benefit to the community of using local suppliers, and the money spent on training that increases the skills of its employees.

It's a very human thing to loudly communicate the positive outcomes and give less voice (or even ignore entirely) the adverse outcomes. This natural bias goes against reporting transparency. It really is in the company's interests to be transparent about all its material outcomes. These are some reasons why:

- Transparency is a part of the accountability responsibility of directors.

- Transparency can inspire trust among stakeholders.

- Clear communication of adverse outcomes can lead to more loyal stakeholders who stand by the company during hard times.

- Radical transparency limits the chance of corporate secrets staying hidden.

Investors and other stakeholders may well already know, or may soon learn, of the adverse outcomes.

It's better to be in charge of the story with proactive communication than to lag behind with a reactive response.

Value creation over time

The company's outcomes on the six capitals are also referred to as value creation over time. The term appeared in the *International <IR> Framework* released by the International Integrated Reporting Council (IIRC).

What can be confusing about the term 'value creation' is that it is often phrased in the positive – 'creation' – even though it encompasses all the outcomes on the six capitals, whether they are positive, adverse or neutral. This has led some companies to refer to positive value creation and negative value creation. Outcomes can also be internal to the company, such as profit and cash flow generated, or external, such as community development. The revised *International <IR> Framework (2021)* uses improved phrasing with the expanded terms of value creation, preservation or erosion. (In 2020, the IIRC decided to do a "light touch" revision of the *International <IR> Framework*. The year long process included the release of three Topic Papers and then a Consultation Draft which were open for public consultation. The process culminated in the *International <IR> Framework* (2021) released in January 2021. For a marked-up copy of the changes in the revised *International <IR> Framework* (2021) see www.integratedreportingsa.org).

Accountants may be inclined to think about value as the financial value set out in the 'Value Added Statement' included in the Annual Financial Statements that shows how the company's annual earnings were distributed among its various stakeholders. It is not this, because the items in the Value Added Statement are monetary payments or allocations to some stakeholders, rather than the positive, adverse or neutral outcomes on the six capitals.

Others might see value creation as shared value (see chapter 2). This term is more accurately used only if all the positive, adverse or neutral outcomes on the six capitals are included, rather than a focus only on the positive outcomes for stakeholders.

A word on corporate social investment (CSI) spend: companies give money and staff hours to sponsoring worthy charitable projects. CSI spend needs to be incorporated into the company's strategy rather than being seen in isolation. For example, providing fresh water to the local community around a mine would be a part of meeting the needs, interests and expectations of that stakeholder group and as such encompassed within the integrated thinking of the mining company.

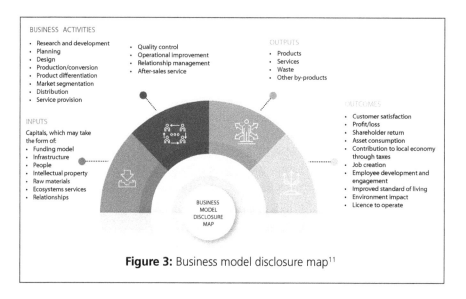

BUSINESS ACTIVITIES

- Research and development
- Planning
- Design
- Production/conversion
- Product differentiation
- Market segmentation
- Distribution
- Service provision

- Quality control
- Operational improvement
- Relationship management
- After-sales service

INPUTS

Capitals, which may take the form of:
- Funding model
- Infrastructure
- People
- Intellectual property
- Raw materials
- Ecosystems services
- Relationships

OUTPUTS

- Products
- Services
- Waste
- Other by-products

OUTCOMES

- Customer satisfaction
- Profit/loss
- Shareholder return
- Asset consumption
- Contribution to local economy through taxes
- Job creation
- Employee development and engagement
- Improved standard of living
- Environment impact
- Licence to operate

BUSINESS MODEL DISCLOSURE MAP

Figure 3: Business model disclosure map[11]

Figure 3 gives examples of possible inputs, business activities, outputs and outcomes. These are determined by the company's business, with the board ensuring that all material amounts are disclosed and, importantly, that the list is complete, covering all six capitals.

Strategy

The company's aim is its purpose. Its business model is the inputs to outcomes process, showing the value creation, erosion or preservation. Strategy is what the company wants to achieve: its strategic objectives and performance targets over the short, medium and long term and how it intends to achieve them.

In setting strategic objectives the board considers all six capitals. This ensures that all factors core to the business are a part of the strategy that is sustainable in the long term. It sees the company maximising its positive outcomes and minimising its adverse outcomes. It also sees the company strategically planning for the future use of resources and relationships that it depends on and cannot do without.

---

[11] CIMA, IFAC, IIRC & PwC *Business Model: Background Paper for <IR>* (March 2013) at www.integratedreporting.org (the figure is adapted from source information).

For example: A gold mine's strategic objectives encompass its four key performance areas, namely, financial returns, environmental and social targets of its social licence to operate, people, and business optimisation.[12] The strategic objectives are based on the company's acknowledgement that in managing potential risks a mine has to maximise its positive outcomes and minimise its negative outcomes. To instil the right behaviour and culture in its workforce, the group performance scorecard is based on performance against targets set for all the strategic objectives. It's a holistic system.

Strategy in our fast-changing world is unlikely to be cast in stone. Directors must stay alert to new threats and opportunities. Good practice dictates that strategy is discussed by the board whenever necessary, but at every board meeting it is considered under the standing agenda item of inputs to outcomes (see chapter 5).

With the fast pace of technological advancement, strategy has to fit into the digital world. Asking whether or not the company's strategy is a digital one is the wrong question. The right question is whether the company's strategy fits into the digital world in which it operates.

Considering the six capitals in strategy and decision-making is known as integrated thinking (see chapter 5).

Companies and the SDGs: A little history

In 2015 the United Nations (UN), together with global companies and civil society, developed 17 Sustainable Development Goals (SDGs). The UN states that the three dimensions of the economy, society and the environment are integrated – and that business is a critical part of the solution. The 17 SDGs aim to achieve sustainable development by 2030, so that we have a chance of an improved society and a sustainable planet by the end of the 21st century.

Many companies show in their reporting which of the 17 SDGs are aligned to their strategy and outcomes[13] and hence how the company is contributing to their country's achievement of the goals. If every company did this, imagine

---

[12] Based on information in Gold Fields Ltd Integrated Annual Report 2016.

[13] Integrated Reporting Committee of South Africa *FAQ: Reporting on the SDGs in the Integrated Report, 2019* at www.integratedreportingsa.org.

the improvement the world would see. And improvement will, as the UN says, strengthen the enabling environment for doing business and building markets around the world.[14] The SDGs make good business sense.

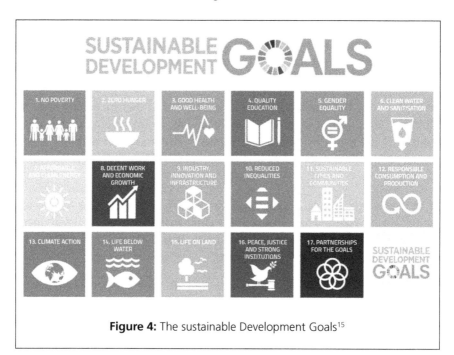

Figure 4: The sustainable Development Goals[15]

The UN's partnership with business has a longer history. In July 2000, the UN launched the ten principles of its Global Compact. The ten principles cover human rights, labour, the environment and anti-corruption. They are derived from the Universal Declaration of Human Rights (1948), the Rio Declaration on Environment and Development (1992), and the International Labour Organisation's Declaration on Fundamental Principles and Rights (1998).

Nelson Mandela's well-known statement is apposite here: 'Action without vision is only passing time, vision without action is merely day dreaming, but vision with action can change the world.'

[14] United Nations Global Compact *How Your Company can Advance the SDGs* at https://www.unglobalcompact.org/sdgs/17-global-goals.

[15] United Nations Department of Public Information at https://www.un.org/sustainabledevelopment/ news/communications-material/.

The vision in 2008 was that the time had come to change corporate thinking and reporting. This gave birth to the *International <IR> Framework* and the concept of integrated thinking and the connectivity of society, the economy and the environment. The Coalition for Inclusive Capitalism, also launched after the global financial crisis of 2008, promoted capitalism as equitable, sustainable and inclusive.

A healthy company is a part of inclusive capitalism.

Chapter 5   Integrated Thinking

Integrated thinking is the knowing and awareness of the reality of the business: all the capitals the company is dependent on and all the effects it is having on them, and the company's understanding and management thereof. It aligns with inclusive capitalism.

Integrated thinking is doing what's best for the company in the long term by knowing the connections.

In musical terms it is like a symphony: one does not have the violinist in one room, the pianist in another room, and so on; rather, they all play together to deliver a symphony. The symphony, in corporate terms, is the business of the company. In a company all the resources and relationships used and impacted must be seen as one.

Integrated thinking can also be described as cause and effect. If an action is proposed (cause) there is consideration of the potential results (effects) on the six capitals. In deciding if the proposed action adds value or not, there is consideration of the effect on the company and the effect on longer-term stakeholder relationships, the company's reputation, the company's risks, and the effect on the availability, pricing and quality of future resources needed.

For example, a chemicals company has the approach that if there are potential adverse effects from a proposed strategy then it will rather forego the proposal and find another route to achieve its aim. Its view is that adverse effects – and the reputational damage and breakdown in stakeholder relationships that they can bring – are not worth the financial gain in the short term and are not in the interests of the long-term health of the company.

Integrated thinking is embedded in strategy once the board determines what outcomes they want the company to achieve for its long-term health and sustainable existence. These desired outcomes are geared to optimise the positive effects on the capitals (including what stakeholders want and expect) and avoid or minimise the adverse ones (including what stakeholders don't want and don't expect).

In ongoing decision-making there are likely to be conscious trade-offs and a balancing of interests over time. This means that after consideration of the potential effects the directors could opt to go with the proposed action, despite it elevating one stakeholder group or capital over others – because the board concludes that it is for the long-term health of the company. This is the board's business judgement call. The board will be aware that its reasons for making the choice will be scrutinised and dissected if ever questioned in court.

Another example of trade-offs and the balancing of interests is a plastics manufacturer. Despite the financial performance of its business, it may opt for change considering the high consumer antipathy to single-use plastics that are seen littering the oceans, the ocean floor and beaches, as well as the threat of new government regulations. After weighing up the likely future scenarios, the board decides to invest financial capital in new manufacturing equipment for recyclable and lighter weight plastic containers that are more acceptable to customers and in turn to consumers. As liquidity is needed for the new plant, no dividends are declared for two years. The board has acted for the long-term health of the company – and a healthy company is beneficial for stakeholders in the long term.

In another example, the board of a bank decides to spend a significant sum on digital banking systems. This dents current financial performance, but it will enable new business, boost customer relationships, help to fend off new competitors, and could lift financial performance in the years ahead.

Integrated thinking moves the company away from a short-term singular focus on profit into a multi-capital approach for a healthy company in the long term. If this sounds like down-to-earth sound management, it is – well-managed companies have applied integrated thinking for years; they just haven't called it such. To other companies integrated thinking may be a 'revolutionary immensity'. The global pandemic of 2020/2021 that affected every country emphasised the connectivity of society, environment and economy and prompted more companies to achieve this awareness and take action.

Integrated thinking also comes into the company's risks and opportunities. Companies experienced in integrated thinking boast an improved risk determination and management process, because it is holistic, covering all six capitals rather than the previous narrow focus of financial risk. They determine risk as anything that could significantly detract the company from its business model and strategy or halt its continued access to important capitals. These experienced boards say there is also much better management of opportunities because every risk usually offers an opportunity to improve and change things for the better. Looking at the plastics company in the example above, it faced the risks of changing consumer views and new government regulations and strategically steered its business to meet its new external operating environment.

A major global research piece on integrated thinking was released by Chartered Global Management Accountants in 2016.[16] The survey questioned 300 C-suite executives and directors from around the world and looked at the effectiveness of decision-making practices in large organisations. The survey revealed that the majority of respondents were battling against bureaucratic decision-making processes, siloed and short-term thinking, a breakdown in trust and collaboration within the organisation, and difficulties with translating ever-expanding volumes of information into knowledge. The survey concluded that the solution to many of these decision-making challenges lies in integrated thinking, because integrated thinking offers the big picture, ensures all relevant insight is available when making decisions, enables analysis of how and why the business is performing in its market drawing on the business model as a powerful frame of reference, and encourages behaviours that build a foundation of trust upon which information is shared and influence secured. In short, the decision-making is better because it is more informed.

 Benefits of integrated thinking are many and include:

- More cohesive approach to decision-making which focuses on value creation in the short, medium and long term.
- Informed strategy that seeks to increase the positive effects and minimise negative effects on the capitals.
- A wider view of risks that reflects the reality of the business.
- Improved understanding of opportunities.
- Deeper understanding of business processes and identification of process gaps.

Figure 5: Benefits of integrated thinking[17]

[16] Chartered Global Management Accountants *Joining the Dots: Decision-making for a New Era* (2016) at https://www.cgma.org/resources/reports/joining-the-dots.html.

[17] Integrated Reporting Committee (IRC) of South Africa *Preparing an Integrated Report: A Starter's Guide* (Updated) (August 2018) at www.integratedreportingsa.org.

Embedding integrated thinking in the company at three levels

It takes a mindset shift for integrated thinking to embed in the company. After all, the focus on financial capital, earnings, profit, sales targets and budgets has been de rigueur for the past century.

Adopting integrated reporting using the guidance of the *International <IR> Framework* is probably the single biggest tip we have for embedding integrated thinking. It's a view based on the experience of companies in South Africa that have been preparing integrated reports for ten years and more. The quality reporters say there is no doubt that the preparation of their integrated reports has enabled and embedded integrated thinking. This stands to reason. The *International <IR> Framework* is, after all, a connecting mechanism: it connects various types of information (financial and non-financial) and the six capitals. For example, the integrated report shows the loop from the important external environment factors to the company's strategy and material matters, it links strategy to risks, and it shows the feedback loop from stakeholders' needs, interests and expectations to strategy, risks, material matters and outlook. And because the *International <IR> Framework* is all about the six capitals there is a complete view of strategy, risks and reporting – all key areas of the board's role. So if the six capitals come into strategy – through maximising the positive outcomes and minimising the negative outcomes – then they automatically fall into the internal reporting and oversight system. Decision-making is similarly holistic, rather than focusing only on the financial.

The mindset shift to the new business model needs to happen at three levels: the board, executives and management, and staff members.

The board

Integrated thinking starts with the board. The board's role and responsibilities lie in four main areas: setting the strategic direction, approving plans and policies, overseeing and monitoring performance, and stewardship and accountability. In doing this it recognises that strategy, risk, performance and sustainability are inseparable.

Step 1 in the shift is getting all directors on the same page – or, stated otherwise, ensuring that the collective mind of the board is a connected and unified one.

Here is an exercise to check the level of unification:

Each director must independently answer the ten questions listed:

1. What is the purpose of the company?

2. Describe how the company created value in previous financial years. Do you really understand what is going on around here?

3. What are the top five external factors impacting the company now or likely to have an impact in the future?

4. Who are the company's stakeholders?

5. What are the legitimate and reasonable needs, interests, concerns and expectations of each stakeholder group? How do they perceive value and is this different to the company's effects on them?

6. How is the company addressing and responding to the above?

7. What resources are used and depended on by the company, and what effects does the company have on them?

8. What risks and opportunities do the stakeholder relationships and resources pose to the company now and in the short, medium and long term?

9. How will the company create positive value in a sustainable manner in the long term and what are its main value drivers?

10. Imagine the company five years after leaving your director's chair. Where do you want the company to be, and will you be satisfied with your role and the decisions made during your tenure?

This discussion by the board is a vital step in integrated thinking to create awareness and consensus. Companies who have carried out this exercise are surprised at how the board hasn't had a unified collective mind. The exercise brings home the reality of the business, which is that the operations, resources and relationships of a company are thoroughly intertwined.

Step 2 is for the board to use its knowledge of how the company uses and affects the capitals (resources and stakeholder relationships) and the associated risks and opportunities to question the company's strategy. Such questioning by some companies has led to a wider determination of the true value drivers of the business, which in turn led to a restatement of the strategic objectives. And a notable extra benefit was better understanding by the board of the business of the company.

Today's board must continually and actively manage the capitals depended on and affected by the company for its long-term health. To ensure it stays informed, the board should have four standing agenda items for meetings:

1. **The inputs to outcomes process:** This enables the board to keep a check on the use and effects the company is having and the implications for the business model, strategy, risks and opportunities, brand and reputation, and prospects.

2. **The quality of stakeholder relationships:** As these relationships are core to the company, knowledge of the state of the relationship and how the company is (or isn't) responding to their needs, interests and expectations can be a warning signal. Furthermore, it gives the board a more informed oversight in regard to management's proposals. The stakeholder information feedback loop is all-important: it would be pointless to have this information and not use it to inform the company's strategy, risks and opportunities.

3. **Resource allocation plans:** As the resources the company depends on are core to the business of the company, plans should be developed to safeguard future access to the resources needed to achieve strategy.

4. **Technology governance and security:** Information systems are the DNA of the business of the company, but they also pose a risk because of the company's dependence and the threat of cybercrime. Disaster recovery, business continuity and cybersecurity are standing points of discussion.

Boards experienced in integrated thinking include integrated information in the agenda packs for meetings – this can include, in addition to the above, performance against targets for strategic objectives and integrated risks. The rationale is that this enables better assessment than the separate silo information previously contained in board packs did. It makes perfect sense for their oversight function, enables more informed decision-making, and aligns information given during the year to that disclosed in the company's annual integrated report (see chapter 10).

Executives and management

While the board strategises, monitors performance, watches risk and generally reflects, it is the task of executives to embed integrated thinking within the company's management, operations and reporting systems. The importance of this task has seen some companies appoint a board committee to oversee integration and monitor progress, with the committee meeting regularly with executives and updating the board at board meetings.

The list of practical points below comes from conversations with executives on what has worked for them in embedding integrated thinking:

1. **Lead from the top.** As one executive says: 'If the CEO is on board then things get done a lot quicker.' If the board is behind integrated thinking, then the CEO certainly should be too. The CEO is the first choice as 'senior champion'; the chief financial officer is also suited.

2. **Reporting influences behaviour.** This is one of the most powerful tools around. Once the board sets strategic objectives based on integrated thinking with targets and key performance indicators (KPIs) for measurement, its performance is included alongside the financial figures in monthly management reports. This continual measurement and monitoring pushes managers to extend their focus beyond the financial and to accept responsibility for delivery. Reporting, active monitoring and consequence management hugely increase awareness of strategic targets. The availability of this holistic information can lead to better decision-making.

3. **Include targets for strategic objectives in individual performance contracts.** While this tool similarly falls into the 'stick' category, it is a powerful driver of change. It ensures responsibility and accountability on an individual level so that behavioural change happens. The 'balanced scorecard' system – a composite of various targets for strategic objectives – is often used. Some companies have filtered the targets first at divisional or departmental level and then into individual performance contracts, thus ensuring that every staff member contributes to and is accountable for the achievement of the company's strategic objectives.

4. **Include targets for strategic objectives in bonus incentives.** This is another of the 'sticks', however, as the manager of a mining company notes: 'This one really works to get people to change as it directly hits their back pocket.' Integrated thinking is a commitment to doing things differently and can require a link to performance-based remuneration that encompasses the holistic strategic objectives rather than only the financial ones.

5. **Create a bonding 'cause'.** This tool is based on people's love of a feel-good story. A good deeds story spreads hope and can create momentum. Relating a strategic objective to a good news story (eg a sustainable fishing supplier's actions result in the revival of a nearly extinct species) can be motivating.

6. **Awareness and understanding of strategic objectives.** Understanding why integrated achievement is important to the company and its future can help whittle down the barriers to change. Explaining the bigger picture, and how each staff member's work fits into it, can be a mindset shifter. Knowing what the company's strategic objectives are can help staff members in their own daily decision-making.

7. **Ongoing internal communication.** Remind, reiterate, reinforce, remind, reiterate, reinforce. One company set its default intranet page to show the strategic objectives and targets and snippets of achievement information.

8. **Small things count.** They really do. Encouraging small changes that are visible in daily working life strengthens the integrated thinking message and acts as a reminder to do things differently. Simple stuff includes swopping plastic water bottles for branded glass water jugs, recycling bins that are easy to access, going paperless and holding video-conference meetings. While these may not be a part of the company's strategic objectives and targets, they can contribute to the mindset change to thinking about the company's effects on society, the economy and the environment.

9. **Enable innovation.** Good ideas for doing things differently, such as improving resources usage, reducing packaging or other ways of achieving the strategic objectives, are often best served up by the people on the floor involved in the process. These good ideas need a channel, though, as they may not always surface unless a system is in place to allow them to rise to the top.

10. **Be seen to do what you say.** If it's clear the actions of executives and management show false commitment to change, then why should employees care? And what does it tell customers and suppliers about the integrity within the company?

11. **Preparing an integrated report.** The preparation of an integrated report with its integrated information and holistic view of the company serves as a powerful tool for integrated thinking (see chapter 10). Experienced reporters say that it's one of the biggest drivers of change in the company.

12. **Open culture.** An open and inclusive culture that enables staff members to challenge mainstream thinking is important.[18]

---

[18] Chartered Global Management Accountants Joining the Dots: Decision-making for a New Era (2016) at https://www.cgma.org/resources/reports/joining-the-dots.html.

Staff members

The ideal is where the board, executives and all staff members are aware of and committed to the company's purpose, ethics, code of conduct, strategic objectives, risks and opportunities, and outcomes – that is, where everybody is in sync and moving in the same direction. That's the ideal!

Efforts need to be made to spread awareness among staff members and ensure that integrated thinking comes into their own decision-making. Those employees who don't walk the talk can pose a reputational risk to the company and bring its integrity into question. One of the tools, in addition to those mentioned earlier, is a one-page document included in the induction pack of new employees that explains all the capitals the company depends on and the effects, along with its strategic objectives.

Employees are also an important stakeholder group to the company. Their perceptions, needs, interests, concerns and expectations, as well as their view of value, should be monitored, with the information included in the stakeholders' feedback and quality of relationship information given to the board.

Integrated thinking is breaking down the traditional silo thinking. It's doing what is in the best interests of the company's long-term health by knowing the connections. It is inclusive capitalism.

Chapter 6   Corporate Revolutions

The company structure we use today is a product of our past thinking.

It is an interesting reflection. Our past thinking was both spurred by inspiration and necessitated by shifts in external conditions, such as the sequence of industrial revolutions and the environmental revolution.

The first industrial revolution, beginning in the late 18th century, harnessed water and steam power to mechanise and speed up production in a move away from the sweat of humans and horses. This new mode of doing things also led to the spewing out of anthropogenic emissions, the adverse environmental effect that society now has to deal with. During this time, the chief mode of doing business was through unincorporated organisations that were owned and financed by wealthy land-owning families. While the wealthy families enjoyed all the benefits of ownership, they took all the risks too, being liable for the claims of creditors and employees on bankruptcy and at risk of losing their shirts and other personal assets.

At the start of the 19th century, the wealthy families were baulking against the 'make or break' liability stakes of ownership. At the same time politicians, being the voice of the people, wanted to see the creation of more jobs (with the concomitant benefit of more votes). Hence, the thinking arose that the government, by passing a statute, could create a new artificial, incapacitated person with limited liability. This would enable the wealthy families to provide financial capital to start businesses and create jobs and that would be the end of any liability or responsibility for them. The artificial person would then be liable for the claims of creditors and employees on bankruptcy. That company structure is still in force today. And the truism remains that society is the effective licensor of the company with the government, as society's representative, having been the creator of the company – hence today's oft-used term 'social licence to operate'.

The creation of the company as an artificial legal person wasn't an easy sell back then. The opposition was fierce, especially among the clergy. In 1844, theologian Lord Thurlow asked: 'Who is mankind to create a person who has no body to be kicked, no soul to be damned and no conscience?'[19] He had a

---

[19] John Poynder (ed) *Literary Extracts from English and Other Works* (1844) 268.

point, for an artificial, immortal and inanimate person has no heart, mind, soul or conscience of its own. Rather, its leaders – the board of directors – of the artificial person, the company, become its heart, mind, soul and conscience. The company structure nevertheless enabled business to flourish, with the second industrial revolution's strides ahead in manufacturing and production processes requiring bigger factories and greater financial capital.

Towards the end of the 19th century, the duties of directors were well established. Their duties were seen as parallel to those of the guardians of an incapacitated human, where the law required them to exercise good faith and loyalty. There was a further duty to take care of their assets: they were to use their skills in the best interests of the incapacitated individual and diligently do their homework to plan for such care over the short, medium and long term. By the start of the 20th century, the limited liability company was the common medium through which to conduct business with its treasured protection of limited liability.

The Ford Motor Company was one such limited liability company. In 1919 the company made an excessive profit ($60 million), leading Henry Ford to announce the plant and machinery would be modernised to manufacture the Model T with greater speed, adding that he would increase the wages of employees as an incentive to work longer hours and weekends to meet the high demand. The Dodge brothers, who were minority shareholders of the company, contended that the company had a duty to pay the excessive profit as a special dividend to shareholders as the primary stakeholders, before increasing the wages of employees.

The Dodge brothers sought a declaratory order that the Ford Motor Company pay out the special dividend ahead of higher wages because of the primacy of shareholders. The court upheld this contention. Consequently, the concept of the primacy of the shareholder and that directors should steer a company to ensure the maximisation of shareholder gains became thoroughly entrenched. Other stakeholders, particularly employees, also started to believe that shareholders were the owners of the company and had primacy over other stakeholders involved in the company such as suppliers, creditors, financiers, communities etc. It's an odd perception, given that shareholders cannot even take a pencil from the company as it doesn't belong to them, and if the company goes into bankruptcy, they are the very last in the queue.

This focus on directors making decisions in the best interests of the general body of shareholders persisted throughout the 20th century. It was famously reinforced by Nobel laureate economist Milton Friedman in the 1970s whose thesis, paraphrased, was that the sole purpose of the company was to make profit without deception. But was that profit at any cost? Did it mean that the company could make a profit while causing adverse effects on society and the environment? And if this was the case, did it mean that society and the environment were subsidising the company's profit? Was this the 'free' part of Friedman's free economy?

By 1970, the third industrial revolution had begun – the computer age. It allowed for faster and slicker production, faster and wider communication, and birthed new skills and industries. It also allowed for a whole lot of new information about companies and insights into what was really happening in the business world. A ground-breaking study of the S&P 500 index at the time showed that a smaller and smaller percentage of market value related to tangible assets on the balance sheet (as determined by financial reporting standards from the International Financial Reporting Standards (IFRS) or the Financial Accounting Standards Board of America (FASB)). The tangible asset percentage shrunk from 83 per cent in 1975 to 19 per cent in 2009.[20]

The plethora of information available about a company has seen the market value (which is in essence the overall view of parties (and algorithms!) external to the company) acknowledge the 'off-balance sheet' worth of the company's intangible assets. Intangibles are patents and copyrights, as well as other intangibles like brands, reputation, ethics, governance, supplier relationships, supply chain issues, limiting adverse effects etc. Ironically, this market value perception was in stark contrast to the internal focus of the company being on financial capital and short-term gains for shareholders. In a deeper irony, while investors gave value to intangibles in the share price, they nevertheless put pressure on the companies to produce ever-rising financial returns. So, while the market value reflected longer-term value, the companies and investors were seeking short-term financial gains. In a later study, it was shown that the percentage of tangible assets in the market value of the S&P 500 index had shrunk even further to 16 per cent in 2015.[21]

---

[20] Ocean Tomo LLC *Intangible Asset Market Value Study* (2009) at https://www.oceantomo.com/media-center-item/ocean-tomos-intangible-asset-market-value-study/.

[21] Ocean Tomo LLC *Intangible Asset Market Value Study* (2017) at http://www.oceantomo.com/intangible-asset-market-value-study/.

At the same time, another revolution was seeding: the environmental revolution. Awareness was growing that the planet had reached ecological overshoot. Companies, as the main users of natural resources, were devouring natural resources faster than nature was regenerating them. There was also the horrible realisation that throughout the 20th century business had been conducted on the crumbling foundation of unsustainable development.

Even more horrible is that much of this was legal, with companies committing 'lawful wrongs'. Directors of companies were striving to maximise shareholder gains – based on a shareholder-centric governance model – even if this was at a cost to society and the environment. So the directors were acting lawfully in their pursuit of profit, but they had caused the innocent company to commit wrongs against society and the environment. It's not that society didn't notice or did nothing. Society's reaction during the 20th century was to ask governments to regulate against the adverse effects, by passing environmental impact laws, and to expect the NGOs to deal with the effects. What the focus should have been on, though, was tackling the source of the adverse effects – namely, how the directors decided the company would make its money and the primacy of shareholders in maximising profit. Society dealt with the symptoms of profit at any cost, rather than the cause.

During the 20th century the ever-rising amount of goods produced brought with it the problem of dealing with discarded waste. Landfills had the double whammy of taking up valuable urban space and toxifying underground water systems. Millions of tons of plastic from manufactured goods have found their way into landfills or rivers, and subsequently into the oceans. Plastic has polluted life below the blue line, exemplified by the infamous 'garbage patch' in the Pacific Ocean, a thrashing island of plastic bottles, containers and bags, twice the size of Texas. The oceans have also been beset by other types of waste carried down by streams and rivers, such as fertiliser chemicals in the industrial farms. The 'dead' zones in the oceans have less oxygen in the water and have caused marine life to flee or die. The oceans have been over-fished by industrial-style trawlers far from their homelands, resulting in unsustainable fishing now being the norm.

The environmental revolution today, however, has to be less about angst and handwringing and more about making the decision to improve things and then taking action. It's finding new ways of doing things, changing behaviour to minimise adverse effects, and focusing on sustainable development in a growing population. The current world population of 7.3 billion is expected to reach 8.5 billion by 2030, 9.7 billion in 2050, and 11.2 billion in 2100.[22]

Nowadays, we're also immersed in the fourth industrial revolution. We have a raft of new tools to make production even faster and slicker and communication even faster and wider. Artificial intelligence, augmented reality, blockchain, drones, the Internet of Things, robotics, virtual reality and 3D printing are the eight essential emerging technologies[23] that will have significant global impact on our business and personal lives in the next ten years. Added to this are the changes in the supply chain, working modes, communication processes, office and manufacturing facilities, and consumer patterns brought about the Covid-19 pandemic.

Doing business and directing a company today requires a mindset change, a new way of thinking. The digital world with its instant and broad communication and radical transparency has brought more equality to stakeholders and conferred power back on society. The environmental revolution has somersaulted companies into innovations in making more with less, and thinking about the medium and long term. This new mindset encompasses purpose, governance, business model and strategy, value creation in a sustainable manner, and understandable reporting.

And strangely, it will take us back to the original intention of the company – being a vehicle that benefits society. Because doing what is in the best interests of the incapacitated artificial person that is the company in the longer term necessitates looking after its intangible assets, its relationships with stakeholders, and the resources it uses – in other words, society.

Another revolution is the change in the role of the accountant. Known as the chief financial officer (CFO), their role has traditionally focused on only the financial aspects of the company. Not so today. As the corporate world has moved away from 'profit without deception' to the process of creating value in a sustainable manner, so too has the role of the CFO.

Their role arises because as CFOs they have had to think about the resources used by the company (dependencies lead to risks and necessitate strategic plans

---

[22] United Nations Department of Economic and Social Affairs *World Population Prospects: The 2015 Revision*, at https://esa.un.org/unpd/wpp/publications/files/key_findings_wpp_2015.pdf.

[23] PwC *The Essential Eight: Your Guide to the Emerging Technologies Revolutionizing Business Now* at https://www.pwc.com/gx/en/issues/technology/essential-eight-technologies.html.

for future access) and the relationships with stakeholders (happy stakeholders, happy company). They have had to think on an integrated basis – the inputs and effects on the six capitals.

The International Federation of Accountants (IFAC) believes that the role of the CFO will evolve into that of a chief value officer (CVO) because of the focus on value creation, preservation or erosion. The CVO's task is to ensure that all aspects of value creation, preservation or erosion are accounted for and communicated to the board so that the board has an informed oversight over any management proposals and any business judgement call that it has to make.

Chapter 7 Good Governance and the Role of the Board

The directors of a company must act with intellectual honesty. They apply responsibility, accountability, fairness and transparency in governing their charge, the company. [24]

Unfortunately, this is not always the case, with a director sometimes falling prey to corporate sins:

> **Greed** – acting out of self-interest.
>
> **Fear** – acting out of self-concern.
>
> **Sloth** – voting with the pack, rather than honestly applying their mind or taking a narrow and short-term view of the true value drivers of the company.
>
> **Pride** – acting too slowly to fix a wrong business judgement call to avoid embarrassment.
>
> **Arrogance** – past successes and a blind belief in the board's long-term strategy breeds arrogance.

In short, committing any of these corporate sins means a director not doing what is in the best interests of the company.

It is hardly surprising that investors are willing to pay a premium for companies that have good quality directors and good corporate governance.

Ethical and effective leadership by the board is the foundation of good corporate governance. In a human the equivalent would be described as good character, moral compass, doing the right thing, and the ability to know right from wrong.

Corporate governance – which can be seen as the 'internal regulation' of the company – is uniquely set by the board itself. This contrasts with the company's 'external regulation', which is the plethora of laws and regulations set by the government, industry bodies, stock exchanges and the like.

---

[24] Mervyn E King *The Corporate Citizen: Governance for All Entities* (2006).

It can be said, though, that the ultimate compliance officer is the company's stakeholders: the telling sign is if stakeholders continue to support the company.

For all the governance practices set in place and applied it really boils down to values: People doing the right thing and making better choices based on sound ethical values that stream through the company and underpin the company's code of conduct.

Typically, a board determines governance by referring to society's latest thinking in this area – as evidenced in the numerous voluntary codes of corporate governance that have surfaced in the past few decades. Interestingly, the creation of a new code of governance has often been sparked by specific events, such as high-profile corporate failures or executive pay scandals. Most of the more recent codes of governance comprise guiding principles, rather than a list of 'thou shalt' rules.

In South Africa, the latest iteration of the *King Codes – the King IV Report on Corporate Governance for South Africa*, 2016 (King IV) – was released by the Institute of Directors in South Africa (IoDSA) in November 2016.[25] King IV has received international acclaim and has been hailed as enlightened thinking as it brought in a focus on governance outcomes, entrenched an 'apply and explain' disclosure approach, and embraced the integrated thinking of the six capitals.[26]

The focus on governance outcomes aims to ensure the 'mindful' achievement of good governance, rather than mindless compliance checks against a list of principles. Four governance outcomes need to be achieved if the board is said to exercise ethical and effective leadership:

- Ethical culture with effective leadership
- Positive value creation in a sustainable manner
- Adequate and effective controls with informed oversight
- Trust and confidence in the company by the community in which it operates with legitimacy of operations.

---

[25] See www.iodsa.co.za.

[26] See Appendix 1 for 'King IV on a Page', an infographic of the governing body's roles and responsibilities and the principles of the Code.

The board can achieve these governance outcomes by adopting King IV's 16 principles[27] and living them through the practices it applies. Each of the 16 principles has recommended practices to apply. If these are not apposite for the company it can adopt other practices to achieve the principle. So, King IV's disclosure approach is to apply the principles and explain the practices.

Integrated thinking is one of the basic concepts of King IV. Integrated thinking comes through in each of the 16 principles and permeates most recommended practices.

The four governance outcomes extend across all the board's primary roles and responsibilities, which are:[28]

- Steering and setting the strategic direction

- Approving policy and planning that give effect to strategy and the set direction

- Overseeing and monitoring implementation and execution by management

- Ensuring accountability for organisational performance by means of, among others, reporting and disclosure.

The board mandates the executives to ensure that its strategy, ethics and values and other governance practices are applied throughout the company.

While the board's governance role is removed from the company's daily operations, the board remains fully accountable for all the actions or omissions of the company. This can be viewed as rather an invidious position, which is why the board must ensure that good governance procedures, processes and practices are in place, such as:

1. Setting and approving the parameters of the company: namely, purpose, business model, strategy, risk management, performance and safeguarding the company's continued status as a good corporate citizen.

2. Appointing and incentivising the right executives to achieve strategy and manage daily operations.

3. Approving the system of internal controls and assurance processes for accurate reporting.

---

[27] Ibid.

[28] IoDSA King IV Report on Corporate Governance for South Africa, 2016 (King IV) 21.

4. Ensuring that external reporting is credible, balanced, complete, accurate and understandable as a part of fulfilling its accountability function.

Furthermore, the board must ensure it gets the information it needs to stay informed throughout the year.

A director wouldn't – and shouldn't – feel comfortable with anything less. This applies even when they have the comfort of directors' liability insurance, because such insurance can never cover the director for reputation lost.

Inclusive governance

The board of a healthy company practises the modern-day inclusive approach to governance. In other words, the board knows and understands the legitimate and reasonable needs, interests and expectations of the stakeholders of the company. The importance of this is that the knowledge allows for the development of strategy and business model on a more informed basis, as well as informing risks and opportunities.

This knowledge comes into the purpose of the company. Stakeholders today want to see that the company's purpose has a dimension of meaning beyond maximising shareholder gains. There is an accumulation of proof on this. Crucially, the board must have a unified collective mind on this, and not a fragmented mind, as the decisions that directors make are guided by this parameter.

At each board meeting there are standing agenda items on stakeholder relationships, the company's inputs to outcomes, and the resource allocation plans. These allow the directors to stay informed on the quality of relationships, the company's dependence on inputs from the six capitals and the effects on the capitals, as well as the plans to ensure access to future resources. The information allows for a more informed oversight over management's proposals – otherwise that oversight is blind. It also alerts to the power that non-financial factors, for example, child labour in the supply chain, can have on the company's financial future. It ensures that the sustainability issues pertinent to the company, such as the conservation of water to a brewery, are treated as part of strategy.

---

[29] World Economic Forum *The Global Risks Report 2019* (14 ed) at http://www3.weforum.org/docs/WEF_Global_Risks_Report_2019.pdf.

Technology governance and security

The fourth industrial revolution necessitates the board having a standing agenda item on technology governance and security. Data fraud or theft and cyber-attacks are among the top five global risks.[29]

The board has ultimate responsibility for technology governance and cybersecurity. It must ensure that the company's information systems are aligned with the business model and strategy. If they are not in alignment, strategy is unlikely to be achieved because information systems are the DNA of a company's business. The executives' responsibility is to ensure that information systems are in place and resilient enough to adapt to the company's strategy; they also have to ensure that information systems are adequately protected from risks such as hacking.

The board has an oversight role over the executives. If the company has a chief information officer, that person should become an executive member of the board so that the board has an informed IT person to help it understand and make judgement calls on IT matters. The range of IT matters discussed by the board is wide, ranging from the protection of private information, which is a statutory requirement in many countries, to security to digital strategy to spending on information systems. The board also has to test whether the company is generating value from its IT investments and will need independent external assurance on the quality of its information systems.

The board will ensure there is a disaster recovery officer, who can also play the role of the data protection officer. The plan for disaster recovery, business continuity and protection of data should be set out in clear, concise and understandable language, the board should approve it, and then have oversight of how it is being implemented. The plan should be assured by an external expert, given its importance.

Because cybersecurity is such a real and big threat to the company, the risk committee should assist the board in this area. If there is not a risk committee, the audit committee can step in.

The board should be asking some specific questions about the company's information systems in regard to cybersecurity strategy and capability to adapt to changes in the security risk environment.[30] The board can also help to advance security posture through a shared vision and culture.

---

[30] The questions have been adapted from PwC Governance Insights Centre *Seven Key Questions your Board Should Ask about Cybersecurity* (January 2017).

- Is our cybersecurity programme aligned with our business strategy?
- Do we have the capabilities to identify and advise on strategic threats and adversaries targeting us?
- Can we explain our cybersecurity strategy to our stakeholders? Our investors? Our ecosystem partners?
- Do we know what information is most valuable to the business?
- Do we know what our adversaries are after or what they would target?
- Do we have an insider threat programme? Is it inter-departmental?
- Are we actively involved in relevant public–private partnerships?

Decision-making: Questions for the board to ponder

The board should make decisions in the best interests of the long-term health of the company. The board must constantly test whether its decisions meet the four outcomes of good governance – and whether it is making decisions that fit within the parameters of the business judgement rule (see chapter 8).

Do we have all the facts to enable us to make a decision? The facts are critical because it is patent that if a board makes a business judgement call without, objectively speaking, having all the facts available, and the call turns out to be one that causes harm to the company, the directors will be liable in damages to the company. In the nature of things, in the boardroom one is dealing with predictions, internal rates of return etc., but the board has to have the facts. The board must be able to separate facts from assumptions, presumptions and submissions.

Do we have all the information we need to make this decision, including plans to access resources needed in the future, and the possible effects on stakeholder relationships in the longer term? Holistic information on the six capitals, from inputs to outcomes, is needed to make a well-rounded decision. If quantitative information is not available, then expert qualitative information is a prerequisite.

Is this a rational business decision at this time, based on all the facts? This is critical. It is not required that a board has a crystal ball and makes the correct business judgement call every time. This is not possible because the board is dealing with uncertain future events. Provided the board applies its mind in an intellectually honest way in the best interests of the company, has no personal financial interest in the matter, objectively has all the facts, and the decision appears to be a rational business decision at that time, the board will be acting in the best long-term interests of the health of the company.

Is this in the best interests of the company? Some decisions may be in the interests of some stakeholders over others, but they are still in the long-term interests of the health of the company. For example, a board may decide not to declare dividends for three years in order to build up liquidity and enable the company to change from a fossil fuel-driven plant to a plant driven by renewable energy. The board opted to build up liquidity rather than increase borrowings because the debt–equity ratio of the company was correctly balanced.

Is our communication to stakeholders transparent? Is it substance over form? Are we telling it as it is, the good with the bad? Is it a balanced communication?

Will the company be seen to be a good corporate citizen and a conscious company by its stakeholders? Will the company be seen to be a healthy one? This is critical in today's world, where society expects and demands much more of companies. The board has to ensure that stakeholders perceive the company as being a long-term healthy one with value being created in a sustainable manner.

Are we being good stewards of the company's assets? Are we taking proper care of the company's assets? Would we be making this decision if those assets were the assets of our family and we were at the head of the family?

A personal question for each director: Do I have any conflict in this matter? The word 'any' is of wide import. By asking the question whether a director has a personal financial interest, the director is giving him- or herself a legal opinion. What is personal and what is financial is not clear-cut. Hence the importance of the word 'any'. A director must disclose any direct or indirect interest and let the board decide whether it is of sufficient importance, from a conflict point of view, that the director should recuse him- or herself from the board meeting.

The foundation of all this is intellectual honesty. The board must put aside any personal interests, past experiences and present needs, and then make a decision in the long-term best interests of the health of the company. This is an intellectual exercise because the board needs to go through the thinking encapsulated in the questions above and ensure that, as a matter of fairness, it is balancing the needs, interests and expectations of stakeholders. In other words, the board must give parity of thinking to the needs, interests and expectations of the various stakeholders but must always make a decision in the best interests of the company.

Chapter 8   Being a Director

In carrying out decision-making at the boardroom table a director must be well-prepared, understand the matter being discussed, ask inquiring questions (even if they are seen to be intellectually naïve) and have a loud voice!

The loud voice matters because directors must have courage – courage to ask the basic questions at the risk of derision or impatience from fellow directors, especially those who are more experienced or who have specific expertise in an area. A director should also 'rid their mind of present needs and past experiences': this means approaching a decision or issue with a clear mind unfettered by outside influence or by those who nominated them as a director.

The mandate of a director is intellectual honesty and a duty of care to the company.

Intellectual naïveté

Fortune magazine, a few years back, published an article on the dumb questions to be asked, especially by non-executive directors. The following is an adaptation of that article:[31]

- How did this company make its money in the year under review?
- Are the company's customers paying up on due date?
- What could really hurt the company in the next few years?
- How is the company doing relative to its competitors?
- If the CEO was headhunted tomorrow, who could assume the position of CEO?
- How is the company going to grow? If by acquisition, how is it going to be financed?
- Is the company living within its means?
- How much do the CEO and other senior executives get paid?

---

[31] Ram Charan & Julie Schlosser 'Ten questions every board member should ask and for that matter every shareholder too. The responses should tell you everything' *Fortune* (10 November 2003) at http://archive.fortune.com/magazines/fortune/fortune_archive/2003/11/10/352828/index.htm.

- What and how are their bonuses calculated?

- What and how does this remuneration relate to the inequality gap with those being paid at the bottom of the corporate ladder?

- How does bad news get to the top? Are the people at the top the last people to hear bad news?

- Do all directors actually understand what is going on around here?

Directors, particularly non-executive directors, must be strong enough to ask intellectually naïve questions. They need to listen to and assess the answers from the executive directors, watching their body language, and then make an independent decision in the best interests of the long-term health of the company.

Legal liability

Each director can be sued for failing to carry out their duties of good faith, care, skill and diligence and which resulted in harm to the company. Failure to use all their skills in the interests of the company can render them liable in damages to the company.

The damages are to the company, rather than directly to the shareholders. However, the shareholders can sue directors on behalf of the company, with any awarded damages being paid to the company itself. If the company is liquidated, the awarded damages will be distributed, along with other net assets, according to the legal ranking of claims against the company (with shareholders being the last in the queue).

While each director independently makes their own decision, they also become a party to the board's collective decision while remaining individually responsible. This means that if a board decision is found to fail the duty of care test, the courts will consider the conduct of each director – as well as their expertise, experience and knowledge of the circumstances of the decision – in deciding whether or not that director is liable to the company for the harm suffered by it. Certain skills, such as financial literacy, are expected of all directors.

The business judgement rule

The business judgement rule has emerged over the years and offers some legal protection to directors. This thinking first started in the USA. It was appreciated that it was inequitable to hold directors liable, especially non-executive directors who had honestly applied their minds but made a business judgement call which, with hindsight, caused harm to the company. There were some necessary conditions for the application of the rule: the director had no conflict of interest; the director had all the facts, objectively speaking, before them at the time; and their decision appears to have been a rational business decision at that time in the circumstances prevailing. The business judgement rule can eradicate or ameliorate the liability of directors.

In some countries, though, there is a statutory conundrum because the corporate statute provides that, if any person breaches any provision of the Companies Act of that country, any person claiming to have suffered harm as a result can claim damages from the person who breached the provisions of the Act, thus allowing directors to be sued. But directors owe their duties to the company and thus it's arguable that such statutory interference with that golden rule does not create a new cause of action against directors.

It stands to reason – and is much better thinking – that directors owe their duty to the company and, if they make a wrong business judgement call, they are held liable for the resulting harm to the company. For example, the directors decide on a business model which is not sustainable, causing a share price drop and loss in shareholders' market value. The shareholders can't claim the loss from directors because the loss is that of the company. In other words, the loss by shareholders in the price of their shares is a reflected loss from the actual loss of the company to which the directors owe their duty of care.

A director will be held liable if a business judgement call causes harm to the company and there was a conflict of interest with personal financial interests; if directors made the call without, objectively speaking, having all the facts before them; or if the decision does not appear to have been a rational business decision at the time and in the circumstances.

Also, if a director acts dishonestly they can be held liable to the company for damages because of their failure to act in good faith. Similarly, if a director acted out of self-interest they can be held liable – this is when they didn't cross the 'self' river, leaving behind self-interest and self-concern – and failed to make decisions in an intellectually honest way and in the best interests of the company. Diligence requires directors to do their homework and understand the issues before the board. To be party to a collective board decision when a director does not understand the issues means the director is failing in their duty of diligence to the company and their duty of care.

FAQs for directors

Q: Can non-executive directors directly question or have direct dealings with management?

Every board should set out a protocol whereby a non-executive director can communicate with management. Usually, this is done through the chair of the board. This formal procedure is necessary otherwise management can become confused as to its reporting line (which is to the CEO) and this can lead to the so-called 'grey' director who is neither non-executive nor executive. The risk of blurred delineation is that the board becomes dysfunctional.

Q: Directors complain that the majority of their meeting time is taken up by compliance issues rather than strategic business issues. Is there a way around this?

Stewardship is an important part of the board's role and responsibilities and stewardship includes ensuring that the company is complying with regulations. Non-compliance is a business risk that can have expensive consequences for the company in the form of penalty fines imposed and reputational damage.

Entrepreneurial-focused directors, especially the founders of the business, can find it frustrating that much board time is spent on compliance. However, compliance matters. Regulations on companies are more likely to increase than decrease as society calls for more authority over companies to prevent errant behaviour and adverse effects. It is unfortunate that the good companies, where behaviour is based on ethical values, have to bear the consequences for their less ethical counterparts.

Some tips to streamline the compliance load: The chair of the board needs to plan for enough time at meetings so that the discussion of strategic business issues is not crowded out by compliance issues. Compliance issues could also be allocated to a board sub-committee to deal with and report back to the board. But, as with any sub-committee, the board cannot abdicate responsibilities and it retains accountability. This means it must interrogate all sub-committee reports before approving them or not.

Q: What makes for a good non-executive director?

Courage – because they have to act in the best interests of the company, which might be contrary to the interests of the shareholder or person who nominated them to the board. They shouldn't need the directorship from the point of view of status or financial compensation. They should have experience of business. They should have courage enough to avoid succumbing to the natural human inclination of not asking questions when they don't properly understand, because they fear that their peers will think they are dim-witted. Indeed, there can be nothing more stupid than a non-executive director being party to a decision when they don't fully understand the matter. They would be failing in their duty of care to the company. They would also be committing a fraud on the company since they have a duty to act with diligence – which, at the very least, requires an understanding of the matter for decision.

The intellectual naïveté of the non-executive director asking questions to clarify something is actually critical to assessing whether management has a clear understanding of the matter under discussion.

Q: Who is regarded as an independent non-executive director?

This is an oft-raised issue. Independence is more a state of mind than the fulfilment of the usual critical bystander tests of, firstly, not being associated with a major supplier, customer or shareholder, and secondly, only receiving from the company the fee for being a non-executive director. The critical bystander tests were developed to differentiate the independent non-executive director from the executive director, who is a manager as well as a director. Every director has the same duties and responsibilities to the company and must show independence of mind.

Q: Incentive-based remuneration: Should directors have 'skin in the game' or not?

This has long been a hot topic, stretching from the days when Bill Clinton, as President of the USA, capped the remuneration of executives. To retain executives, the concept of share options granted by the company to executives came into being. The bull run on stock markets thereafter resulted in executives receiving huge pay-outs when they sold their option shares – much to the displeasure of society.

The corporate belief was that the granting of share options to executives would result in their thinking being aligned with the thinking and needs of shareholders.

In reality, this was an error and a mismatch. Over the years, shareholders have held listed company shares for an ever-decreasing time period. Nowadays, on average, they can hold shares for no longer than six months. Electronic trading has seen share ownership change within 25 seconds. The shareholders of listed companies have become transient. This was the great mismatch. Executives with a three- to five-year contract should have been looking at the long-term health of the company rather than looking after the short-term wealth of transient and short-term shareholders.

Today's better thinking is that non-executive directors do not receive share options; if executive directors receive share options, they are included in their variable remuneration package. Variable remuneration, as recommended in King IV, requires that the remuneration sub-committee of the board incentivise management to achieve all three of the critical dimensions for sustainable development (the economy, society and the environment). Here is an example of how this can work: the target for a bonus pay-out is set at a 7 per cent increase in earnings. The target was exceeded and the executive is paid one-third of the calculated bonus. But in that year there were also adverse effects on the environment. The executive then needs to furnish five targets as to how they intend to eradicate or ameliorate the adverse effects. If these targets are achieved in the year ahead, then they are paid out another one-third of the bonus. The same approach is taken in regard to the effects on society relating to the last third of the bonus. And if there were positive effects on the environment and society, they should furnish five targets as to how they are going to enhance those positive outcomes.

If, as a result, the CEO earns what *prima facie* appears to be a huge amount of remuneration it is much more palatable to stakeholders that the executive was incentivised to drive the company towards long-term health and that there were positive outcomes on society and the environment.

Nothing prevents an executive or a non-executive director from putting their hand into their pockets and out of their own money buying shares in the company in which they are directors. Having skin in the game can help them to focus on making decisions in the best long-term interests of the company.

Q: Who gets sued, the directors or the auditors?

When there is a corporate collapse the liquidator usually sues the auditors – because they are seen to have the deepest pockets as the auditor is obliged to have prudential insurance cover. Directors also often carry directors' and officers' insurance cover for decisions made in good faith. If the decision is made out of dishonesty or self-interest, of course, the insurance cover will not assist the director.

A director gets sued when they have failed to carry out their duties of good faith, care, skill and diligence. An auditor will get sued if they have failed to properly apply an international standard of auditing or have done so negligently.

The auditor is appointed by a contract and, in breaching that contract, the auditor has absolute liability to the company. The liability is joint and several with other wrongdoers, but in many countries the auditor is unable to join those other wrongdoers and ask for apportionment of the loss. In some countries the auditor is able to ask for apportionment of loss as between the company and the auditor, for example, if the CFO went rogue. But this is more illusory than real because the company itself has not been the cause of, for example, the auditor's opinion not being properly done. It is rather the fault of its corporate leaders, given that the company is incapacitated and not able to ensure that the necessary information is given to the auditor timeously or qualitatively.

It would be extraordinary if a court were to find that the sole cause of the collapse of a company was the failure of the external auditor to apply an international standard of auditing properly or that they did so negligently. There is, as a matter of fact, always a conglomeration of acts or omissions of other joint wrongdoers causing the collapse of a company. This could be the chief operating officer going rogue or a parts supplier for the company's product supplying faulty parts. Fairness demands that the auditor should be able to join these wrongdoers and ask the court to apportion blame between them.

As is the case with the business judgement rule applying to directors, an auditor judgement rule is being discussed internationally. If an auditor complied with the code of conduct of their regulatory body, had no financial interest conflict, and honestly applied the international standards of auditing to the best of their ability, and on the audit evidence it was rational to give an unqualified audit opinion at that time, the auditor should, like a director, escape liability.

Chapter 9   The Chair of the Board

The chair is the leader of the board while the chief executive officer is the leader of the executives and management team implementing the decisions of the board. Boards think, reflect and monitor, whereas management does. These are two different functions – which is why the role of chair and the role of the chief executive officer should not be combined in one person.

The chair is elected by the directors who, in turn, have been elected by the shareholders at an annual general meeting.

There should not be a split of authority and responsibility. Hence, the chair should not be elected by major shareholders in terms of the company's Articles of Association or Memorandum of Incorporation. A representative shareholder, such as the government of the day, should not appoint the chair of the board of a state-owned company. If the government does so, the chair sits in the board meeting with two pips on their shoulder: one as leader of the board and the other as representative of the sole shareholder. This throws out the balance in boardroom discussions and results in a lack of creative tension.

The chair is responsible for the effectiveness of the board. The board is at the apex of the corporate architecture and is responsible for ethical and effective leadership.

What makes for a good chair of the board?

Friendly but not too friendly: Although the chair is a member of the team – and therefore collegiate – they have to learn to be a bit arm's length from fellow directors. This is important. At times the chair may have to ask a director to resign for reasons of dishonesty or for not giving material input to the decision-making process. And at times the chair may be a party to dismissing the chief executive officer who is also a director. This is one of the most difficult things for the chair to manage: being collegiate and at the same time being arm's length from the individual directors making up the board.

Listening skills: The chair must be a good listener – and the last person to speak at meetings. They must be able to summarise a lengthy debate and suggest that the meeting is inclining towards a certain decision. They must endeavour to obtain a consensual business judgement call at all times. They must be able to draw the threads of the discussion together to weave a fabric which can be looked at through a legal microscope. Importantly, the chair must ensure that this appears in the minutes of the meeting. The minutes must reflect that the board had applied its mind to the facts at the time and made a rational business judgement call in the circumstances at that time. This is critical, so that directors are able to refresh their memories from the minutes years down the line if they are ever sued for a failure of duty of care and want to raise the business judgement rule as a defence.

Encourage questions – and be a body language expert: The chair should encourage directors, especially the non-executives, to ask the intellectually naïve questions. Experienced chairs say that it is useful to watch the body language of the executive directors in answering those questions as it can sometimes help to assess what they really think of a proposed action.

Encourage independent thinking: A chair should constantly test the independence of thinking of the directors. Are they making their own decisions or following the herd? Directors, in turn, should constantly assess the independent thinking of the chair, their leader. The chair, like other directors, must have crossed the 'self' river into the area of intellectual honesty.

Ensuring the board has a kaleidoscope of skills: The chair's task is to ensure that there is a kaleidoscope of different skills on the board. For this reason, the chair should also be the chair of the board's nominations committee. This committee can recommend to shareholders the appointment of a person with certain skills which the chair believes would add to the quality of business judgement calls made by the board.

Watching out for business viability: The chair must ensure that the board has applied its mind to the sustainability issues pertinent to the business of the company, that these have been embedded into the company's business model and strategy, and that plans are in place for any adverse outcomes on the six capitals to be eradicated or ameliorated and the positive outcomes on the capitals enhanced.

Getting the board to have a unified mind on the external perceptions of the company: A useful exercise is for the chair to write up the characteristics of the company as perceived by external stakeholders and then discuss these offline with directors and management. The aim is to get awareness and agreement by all. The characteristics of the company are different to its culture: the characteristics of a company rather than its internal culture are perceived by stakeholders, and if a board decision is inconsistent with those perceptions, it must be explained by the company.

Tapped in and tuned in: The chair has to be plugged into politics, technological advancements, environmental issues and business issues on a global basis. For while the world is physically round, companies operate in a flat, borderless electronic world.

Values: The chair is the guardian of the company's values and should conduct themselves in a responsible manner. The chair is often seen to create the image of the company, whether it is or isn't a responsible corporate citizen, and if it is operating as a healthy company. They must therefore conduct themselves accordingly and, if possible, be a person of stature in the community in which the company operates.

Reporting: The chair should ensure that all reports emanating from the company are balanced, in the sense of the good with the bad. The natural human inclination is to highlight the positives and downplay the negatives, and the chair should ensure that this never happens.

Being a confidant to the CEO: The relationship between the chair and the chief executive officer should be one of trust and confidence. This is particularly so in the case of a listed company, where the chief executive is unable to talk freely to others about matters which are not in the public domain as they would be in breach of securities legislation and risk insider trading. Consequently, the chair becomes the chief executive's confidant – all the while though being friendly, but not too friendly.

If the relationship between the chair and the chief executive officer breaks down, the balance in the boardroom is disrupted.

When the chief executive officer and the management team implement a business judgement call by the board which is very successful for the company, the spotlight will fall on the chief executive officer. But when there is a corporate failure – in the sense that the chief executive officer has to the best of their ability attempted to carry out the decision of the board but it turns out to be a bad business judgement call – the chair should, figuratively speaking, be holding the chief executive's hand to dilute the media pressure on them.

Running the board meetings

Venue of meetings: The chair ensures the place of the meeting is suitable. The meeting table should be oval in shape so that directors can clearly see and hear each other. The boardroom is usually fitted with video and telephonic conference facilities, which means there is no reason why a director should not participate at a board meeting.

The agenda: The chair should ensure the agenda covers all pertinent matters in addition to the four standing agenda items, as discussed in chapters 4 and 7.

Management reports: The chair should ensure that the management reports presented to the board are in clear, concise and understandable language and do not contain in-house jargon developed by management. When necessary, a glossary of industry technical terms can be attached to management reports to assist directors' understanding.

Ensuring non-executive directors understand the issue: Directors obviously have to understand the management report on a critical issue. Prior to the meeting, the chair will communicate with one of the non-executive directors who they know has skill and experience on the issue and ask them to research the issue further. The chair will then ask that director to lead the discussion at the meeting. The rationale for this is that the discussion starts off at a more informed level and hopefully a better business judgement call will be made by the board.

To ensure that directors have a thorough understanding of the issue, the chair should test this from time to time. Here is an example: a 30-page management report on a particular issue is to be discussed at the board meeting. Before getting into the discussion, the chair asks if the management report can be taken as read and understood. The issue is then discussed for say 45 minutes, leading the chair to ask if everyone is resolved in a certain direction. Assuming that all directors answer in the affirmative, the chair will then select one director and ask them to explain in some detail why they have voted in the affirmative. If that director hasn't really understood the management report and hasn't followed the 45-minute discussion, they will struggle to motivate their answer. This tool helps the chair have better control of the board and ensures there is a creative tension in the boardroom. It also ensures that directors do their homework. Directors have to diligently strive to understand the board pack. If they don't, they fail in their duty to the company because they should be its heart, mind and soul.

Ensuring all the facts are on hand: The chair must ensure, objectively speaking, that all the facts are before the board. This is critical because of the business judgement rule and the reality that if, objectively, more facts could have been obtained at that time and the decision turns out to be a poor business judgement call causing harm to the company, then the directors will incur liability.

Running the meeting: The chair should ensure that a board meeting does not continue for more than three to five hours. If the meeting takes longer it means the chair has not ensured that management reports are in an understandable language; or they don't have enough control over the board to ensure that reports were understood prior to the meeting to avoid going through them page by page; or they haven't created a situation where directors are kept on their toes and where directors talk through the chair rather than debating issues across the table.

It is important for the chair to realise that a board meeting is a dynamic event: they will not know in advance the outcome of discussions to be made and the inputs from various directors with different backgrounds and different skills.

Productivity: The chair's task is to ensure that time is productively spent at meetings. They need to prepare well in advance of the meeting, including discussing the objectives of the meeting with the chief executive, the company secretary, and/or the financial director and chief information officer.

Linking to the audit committee: The chair should liaise with the chair of the audit committee and discuss with them the reports received from the head of internal and external audit.

Evaluating the board's performance

The chair should ensure the board's performance is evaluated at least once every two years. This time interval gives the board opportunity to correct any deficiencies recorded in the evaluation. Individual directors should also be evaluated, as should the chair.

The chair's role is absolutely important in the 21st century where we have moved from a shareholder-centric governance model to a company-centric one. The chair must be certain that the board has understood that it is the conscience of the company. The company will or will not be seen to be a healthy one according to the effectiveness of the board, the quality of the company's business model and its strategy on the adverse and positive effects on the six capitals, and its business judgement calls.

Chapter 10 The Integrated Report

The purpose of the company is its aim; the business model is its inputs to outcomes process; the strategy is its goals and how it deals with positive and negative outcomes – all are integrated. It stands to reason, then, that the company's prime external communication – the annual report – should be an integrated report.

The official definition of an integrated report is *a concise communication about how an organisation's strategy, governance, performance and prospects, in the context of its external environment, lead to the creation of value over the short, medium and long term.*[32]

More simply put, it's a short, sharp read giving material, concise and complete information about the company's purpose, external environment, business model, strategy, risks and opportunities, performance, outlook and governance. It offers a holistic understanding of the company. As the company's primary external report it is positioned as the 'first read' or 'umbrella report' after which users can access more detailed information, for instance, the Annual Financial Statements, the Sustainability Report, the Remuneration Report, and other supplementary or compliance reports – all of which can appear on the company's website.

Using the analogy of the octopus in explaining the corporate reporting suite, the integrated report is the head of the octopus with all other reports linking to it through the arms of the octopus. Some organisations adopt a horizontal octopus approach, with the integrated report being the front section of a longer report which includes the Annual Financial Statements. (Smaller organisations usually opt for this approach.)

The integrated report is not a new concept. The term appeared in King III in 2009 and before that a few global companies had disclosed integrated information in their annual reports, recognising that this served them better than the siloed information of separate reports.

The integrated report can fit within the legislation and regulations in different countries. For instance, the Strategic Report[33] released by larger companies in

---

[32] International Integrated Reporting Council *International <IR> Framework* at www.integratedreporting.org.

[33] The requirement for a Strategic Report appears in the UK Companies Act 2006.

the UK contains integrated information and can be said to be an integrated report in all but name. Likewise, in Japan, the METI's *Guidance for Integrated Corporate Disclosure*[34] deals with value creation for the organisation and other stakeholders and future orientation. The Australian Securities & Investment Commission, in its regulatory guide 247,[35] wants information set out which assesses an entity's operations, financial position, strategies and prospects for future financial years. The *Management's Discussion and Analysis of Financial Position and Operational Performance*[36] Topic 9 of the Financial Reporting Manual of the US Securities and Exchange Commission requires commentary to enhance the financial disclosure and provide the context within which financial information can be analysed. It's clear that the need for integrated information, which shows the connections between the financial and the non-financial, is driving the directional push.

The world's financial standard-setters are also seeing the need (and have become a driving force) to give financial statements better context and to show the connections between financial and non-financial information. It's an interesting acknowledgement of the insufficiency of financial statements – or that the financial statements do indeed cover only a single slice of the cake. The road ahead looks set to entrench the integrated report as a company's primary external report showing the links between the financial and non-financial over the short, medium and long term. And the *International <IR> Framework* can be the international best practice guidance to use.

The year 2020 will be renowned as the year of the global pandemic. It was also the time when the global financial standard-setters and the main sustainability reporting organisations made game-changing moves to achieve a greater blend of financial and non-financial information in corporate reporting. The International Integrated Reporting Council (IIRC) started the ball rolling with the announcement that it would work with sustainability organisations - the GRI, Sustainability Accounting Standards Board (SASB), Carbon Disclosure Project (CDP) and the Climate Disclosure Standards Board (CDSB). A few months later, the IIRC announced its intention to merge with the US-based SASB to form the Value Reporting Foundation. In keeping with the global

---

[34] The Ministry of Economy, Trade and Industry (METI).

[35] Regulation 247 *Effective disclosure in an operating and financial review* at https://asic.gov.au/regulatory-resources/find-a-document/regulatory-guides/rg-247-effective-disclosure-in-an-operating-and-financial-review/.

[36] At https://www.sec.gov/corpfin/cf-manual/topic-9.

mood for change, the IFRS Foundation (the custodian of the International Accounting Standards Board (IASB)) announced it would look into forming a Sustainability Standards Board (SSB) to sit alongside the IASB. Its role being to develop international standards for sustainability information that would result in global comparability and smooth the reporting path for preparers and users.

Companies listed on the Johannesburg Stock Exchange (JSE) in South Africa have issued the most integrated reports, as they have been doing so since 2010.[37] It's inspiring to note that, quite apart from the external reporting advantages of integrated reports, a benefit frequently cited by these companies is that it prodded them into integrated thinking. It's an extremely useful internal management tool, they say, in recognising the company's dependence on all six capitals and the resulting effects it is having. Other notable benefits include a better understanding of the business model, broader risk management that encompasses the six capitals, and the alignment of internal and external reporting. The latter is truly significant as companies have for eons strived to better match their internal reporting with external reports.

Today, integrated reports are prepared by many companies in many different countries. A global research study of integrated reporting and integrated thinking by Black Sun[38] reveals similar benefits: it connects departments that have been working in silos, and improves internal processes leading to a better understanding of the business, increased focus and awareness of senior management on the business model, better articulation of strategy, and management awareness of the importance of creating value for all the company's stakeholders.

---

[37] See the block below for more on the history.

[38] Black Sun Plc Realizing the Benefits: *The Impact of Integrated Reporting* (2014) at https://integratedreporting.org/wp-content/uploads/2014/09/IIRC.Black_.Sun_.Research.IR_.Impact.Single.pages.18.9.14.pdf.

Some of the benefits of preparing integrated reports cited by experienced South African reporters are:

INTERNAL

- Critical thinking about the business and the positive and negative value it creates
- A good management tool
- An organisation-wide focus on environmental, social and governance matters that are core to the organisation and its future, including improved data quality
- Improved risk management
- Improved knowledge-management processes and information for decision-making
- Focused integration of key performance indicators (KPIs), risks, and strategic objectives determined after consideration of all material capitals
- Breaking down internal silos and promoting sharing of information in the organisation
- Greater alignment of internal and external reporting

EXTERNAL

- Disclosure of strategy gives context to performance and outlook
- More future-focused information
- Clear depiction of the business model increases understanding of the value creation process
- Succinct and connected reporting is easier to interpret and analyse
- Improvement in balanced reporting and transparency through:
  - providing information about all material capitals;
  - positive and negative performance and outcomes; and
  - addressing both historic performance and future outlook.
- Improves quality of communication between the organisation and stakeholders that can set the foundation for trust and legitimacy
- Reduces information asymmetry

Figure 6: Benefits of the integrated report from experienced reporters[39]

---

[39] Integrated Reporting Committee (IRC) of South Africa *Preparing an Integrated Report: A Starter's Guide (Updated)* (August 2018) at www.integratedreportingsa.org.

The integrated report is owned by the board, and is regarded as the board's 'voice'. As such, it shouldn't be seen as a glossy PR document put out by the marketing department, but rather as a part of the board's duty of accountability through transparent and balanced reporting.

The guidance to use

International best practice is to use the *International <IR> Framework* (*<IR> Framework*).[40] In 2020, there was a "light touch" revision and the *International <IR> Framework (2021)* was released - the changes are not extensive, see integratedreportingsa.org. The <IR> Framework is a voluntary code released by the global body, the International Integrated Reporting Council (IIRC), in December 2013. The IIRC's members are a who's who of international reporting organisations, such as the International Accounting Standards Board, the GRI, the Sustainability Accounting Standards Board, the International Corporate Governance Network, the World Business Council for Sustainable Development, the International Organisation of Stock Exchanges, and multinational companies and institutional investors.

The <IR> Framework is principles-based, enabling it to be applied by profit and non-profit organisations and in the private and public sector. The fundamental concepts underlying the <IR> Framework are the six capitals, integrated thinking and value creation. There are 19 requirements that form the basis of the <IR> Framework and should be met if an integrated report is stated as being in accordance with the <IR> Framework. These 19 requirements comprise seven Guiding Principles (they define the nature of information suitable for the report); eight Content Elements (information areas that offer a structure for the report); a statement of responsibility by the governing body; a statement of accordance with the <IR> Framework; and that the report is a 'designated, identifiable communication'. Figure 7 below lists the 19 requirements of the <IR> Framework.[41]

---

[40] At www.integratedreporting.org or www.integratedreportingsa.org.
[41] Refer to the *International <IR> Framework* to obtain more information on the requirements.

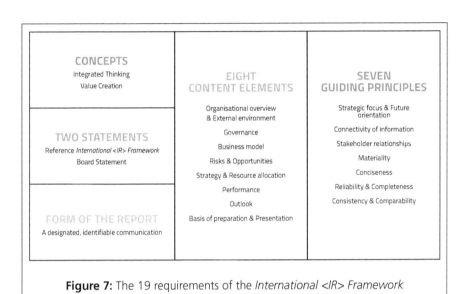

CONCEPTS	EIGHT CONTENT ELEMENTS	SEVEN GUIDING PRINCIPLES
Integrated Thinking Value Creation	Organisational overview & External environment	Strategic focus & Future orientation
TWO STATEMENTS Reference *International <IR> Framework* Board Statement	Governance Business model Risks & Opportunities Strategy & Resource allocation	Connectivity of information Stakeholder relationships Materiality Conciseness
FORM OF THE REPORT A designated, identifiable communication	Performance Outlook Basis of preparation & Presentation	Reliability & Completeness Consistency & Comparability

Figure 7: The 19 requirements of the *International <IR> Framework*

The board statement

One of the significant requirements is the statement of responsibility[42] for the integrated report from the board (or governing body of the organisation). This statement entrenches the board's ownership of the report, acknowledging the board's responsibility for the integrity of the report, and its opinion on whether the report meets the requirements of the <IR> Framework. A new addition in the updated *International <IR> Framework (2021)* is the encouragement of the disclosure of the processes, systems and key roles and responsibilities in the preparation of the integrated report as supplementary information to the statement.

While the <IR> Framework requires adherence to its 19 requirements, some leeway is given for new reporters for full adherence in the *International <IR> Framework (2021)*. There is acknowledgment that integrated reporting is a journey and that meeting all 19 requirements may not be achieved in the early years of adopting the <IR> Framework. In this instance, listing the requirements not achieved and the reasons why is recommended disclosure.

---

[42] *1G Responsibility for an integrated report, International <IR> Framework*. If local legal regulations preclude the inclusion of this statement, there is allowed alternative disclosure, which is an explanation of the processes and systems in place to ensure the integrity of the integrated report.

It is suggested, given the fast pace of change and heightened uncertainty in today's world, that the board statement be dated, showing the exact date of approval of the integrated report by the board.

A useful resource for those new to integrated reporting is *Preparing an Integrated Report: A Starter's Guide (Updated)*.[43] This practical Guide sets out where and how to start. Figure 8 at the end of this chapter is from the Guide and shows the information flow and reporting process. A useful resource for all preparers is the *Delivering a Meaningful and Concise Integrated Report: An Information Paper* which sets out six particular focus areas for the report.[44]

Appendix 1 gives the *International <IR> Framework (2021)* showing the eight Content Elements and their suggested content. The order of the Content Elements is entirely flexible and is determined by the company in best explaining its process of value creation, erosion or preservation. Typically, a report can be logically structured as follows: about the report or introduction; organisational overview; the main external environmental factors affecting the company; its material matters; the business model diagram followed by the stakeholders relationship table; the strategic objectives and targets for the short, medium and long term; the risks and opportunities; performance against the strategic objectives; the outlook for achieving the strategic objectives in the future; and governance. A logical structure for the report enhances readability by keeping the report concise but complete, and it minimises duplicate information. (The aim is to state information once in a report with cross-references back to the initial explanation or disclosure.)

FAQs for directors and executives

Q: What happens if the company doesn't have information systems to provide information for the integrated report (ie there is a lack of reliable information)?

Systems need to be in place to collect and manage reliable financial and non-financial information. The latter may have to be implemented and there could be cost considerations. However, such information will serve the

---

[43] Integrated Reporting Committee (IRC) of South Africa Preparing an Integrated Report: A Starter's Guide (Updated) (August 2018) at www.integratedreportingsa.org.

[44] Integrated Reporting Committee (IRC) of South Africa, *Delivering a Meaningful and Concise Integrated Report: An Information Paper* at www.integratedreportingsa.org

company well – after all, it is core to the business (the whole of the cake with financial information being a single slice of the cake). It is decision-relevant information and can result in more informed decision-making through the availability of holistic information. In other words, it is information that the business should have anyway, operating as it does in a connected world.

Lack of systems shouldn't deter a company from making a start on its integrated report because some of the information needed for the report may already be accessible, for instance, the major factors in the external environment (a weak economy, new regulations affecting the industry, global issues such as a pandemic and climate change); information on strategy, risks and opportunities; and governance practices and information.

The <IR> Framework allows for two exceptions whereby material information can be excluded from the integrated report. The first exception caters for a lack of reliable information – and in this instance, the alternative disclosure requirements are to explain the nature of the information, the reason why it's unavailable, the steps being taken to get it, and the expected timing. This exception also covers the instance where inclusion of the information is legally prohibited (eg an ongoing legal case). The second exception relates to the somewhat thorny issue of giving away competitive information (see below).

Q: 'Opening the kimono' – will too much competitive information be revealed?

Directors may be concerned about having a tell-all on strategy or other information in the report that could be used by competitors. The <IR> Framework allows for such exclusion as the second exception referred to in the question above.

The board's judgement comes into play here. Clearly, it's better for the company if stakeholders (as users of the report) understand the direction of the business and the company's messaging. At the least, information in the report should not be less than that disclosed in investor presentations, and useful strategic information can be given at a high level and not as detailed information on how a particular strategic objective will be carried out.

An experienced chairperson of listed companies describes it this way: 'We aim for transparency. To us, competitive information would be in giving the gross margins on our various products or giving the detailed implementation plans for strategy.'

Q: How can the board ensure that the report's preparation process catches all the material matters and information that ought to be disclosed, ie that the report is complete and in pursuance of the directors meeting their duty of accountability?

Materiality is key to any form of reporting as it ensures that what matters most is disclosed. Different reporting standards have different determinations of what is material – so financial reporting materiality is not the same as that for sustainability reporting. For the integrated report, the information that matters most is that which affects the company's value creation, erosion or preservation process. The <IR> Framework defines a material matter thus: *A matter is material if it could substantively affect the organisation's ability to create value in the short, medium or long term.*[45] Typically, it's a matter that can have a significant effect on strategy, governance, performance or prospects – seen through the dual lens of six capitals and time (short, medium and long term).

Given the importance of the materiality determination process – after all, junk in, junk out – the <IR> Framework has a requirement to explain the process in the report: *How does the organisation determine what matters to include in the integrated report and how are such matters quantified or evaluated?* The board needs to approve this process for thoroughness and have oversight to ensure that all the material matters and information are included in its report. The completeness of the process should be beyond doubt because it will be scrutinised by users of the integrated report.

A question that new reporters ask is how the material matters resulting from the determination process differ from the company's risks. The answer lies in their determination processes. If the risk process includes all six capitals (from inputs to outcomes) and time (short, medium and long term) then the only main difference is that the materiality determination process might have identified some actual events in the year (eg a cyber or viral attack) or identified some opportunities as material matters. However, if the risk process was limited to financial risks only (an outdated process!) then the broader materiality process would have spewed out material matters relating to all six capitals; the short, medium and long term; and component factors of the value creation process such as a weakening relationship with a key stakeholder group.

A point to note: A few experienced reporters in South Africa adopt an alternative view of materiality, which we have called the 'whole darn thing': in this instance,

---

[45] *International <IR> Framework*, Glossary at 33.

the company states that all information in the report is considered material (as opposed to giving a separate list of say ten identified material matters). This view is technically acceptable but really is more suited to experienced reporters in order to counter the risk of the integrated report not being complete – and the board should explicitly state that it is comfortable that all material matters have been addressed in the report.

Q: What future-oriented information is typically disclosed in the report?

The <IR> Framework calls for strategic and future-oriented information (as a Guiding Principle) and there is a specific Content Element for Outlook. In the early days of integrated reporting, directors were concerned that such information was tantamount to a profit forecast and related to financial performance. It is not. What the <IR> Framework calls for is information relating to the company's value creation, erosion or preservation process that is future-oriented and strategic in nature. This is an important Guiding Principle and steers companies away from reporting on only historical performance and information in the report. The Outlook Content Element focuses on the leadership's view of the main uncertainties and challenges facing the company in achieving its stated strategic objectives and targets in the future. Such information would include a description of the uncertainties and challenges and the possible implications for the company. Some examples are expected changes in the industry, regulations, natural environment, consumer trends and relevant global factors affecting the company. The leadership's view and explanation of the possible implications should be substantiated, rather than vague and general: for instance, by giving scenario analysis, lead indicators, the assumptions used in projections etc. As you may have guessed, much of this information may already be disclosed in the integrated report in the external environment, material matters, risks and opportunities and in the reviews by the chair, the CEO and the CFO. To enhance readability for users, it's a good idea to include in the report a summary of the information already given, with cross-references to where the information appears in the report. And as a check for completeness of information, the company should ask itself the question in the Outlook Content Element: *What challenges and uncertainties is the organisation likely to encounter in pursuing its strategy, and what are the potential implications for its business model and future performance?*[46]

---

[46] The IRC of South Africa has a useful information paper on outlook: *Reporting on Outlook in the Integrated Report: An Information Paper* at https://integratedreportingsa.org/reporting-on-outlook-in-the-integrated-report/.

Q: Are directors legally liable for the integrated report?

In many jurisdictions, directors have a duty of accountability which encompasses accurate and transparent reporting. It is a matter of legal consequence that directors are responsible for the integrated report – whether or not the integrated report includes the statement of responsibility required by the <IR> Framework.[47]

Q: Can the integrated report be assured?

The international standard-setter, the International Auditing and Assurance Standards Board, is addressing this issue and the standards that can be used. One of the challenges to external assurers is that the integrated report contains subjective information, for instance, the material matters and their completeness, and future-oriented information. It is likely, though, that given the responsibility directors have for the report, assurance on the full integrated report will soon be commonplace.

Q: Why does the reporting boundary of the integrated report differ from the financial reporting boundary?

The boundary of the integrated report is logically wider because it covers the company's inputs and outcomes on the six capitals, some of which are owned by the company and some of which are not. The financial reporting boundary, by contrast, is defined by ownership and financial accounting standards. View the financial reporting boundary as the core, and add to that the risks, opportunities and outcomes to the company that may arise from external stakeholders and entities.

If the boundary of the integrated report is limited to the financial reporting boundary then it is unlikely to be complete in terms of disclosure of the material matters and information.

Q: Is the integrated report only for larger companies or should SMMEs be doing it too?

Experienced reporters have said that one of the biggest benefits of preparing integrated reports is that it's an extremely useful management tool in better understanding their company: from the dependence and effects on the six

---

[47] The IRC of South Africa has a useful information paper on the need for balanced reporting: *Achieving Balance in the Integrated Report: An Information Paper* at https://integratedreportingsa.org/achieving-balance-in-the-integrated-report/.

capitals, to a broader view of risks and opportunities. This is a benefit available to SMMEs. In today's connected world, sticking to the old-fashioned way of doing things can be the real risk to their business.[48]

Q: How does the integrated report relate to integrated thinking in the company?

Using the analogy of an iceberg: the integrated report is the tip of the iceberg with integrated thinking being the body of the iceberg, ie the way the company is governed and managed.

A Little History – The Integrated Report

The integrated report is a 21st century phenomenon. In 2002, *the King Report on Corporate Governance for South Africa 2002* (King II) recommended 'integrated sustainability reporting' by organisations to stress the impact of the financial on the non-financial and vice versa. In 2006, the Danish healthcare group Novo Nordisk reported on its connected financial and sustainability information. Some other big-name companies, such as Philips, Natura and Southwest Airlines, also started releasing integrated information reports.

In 2009, companies and other organisations in South Africa were called upon to prepare an integrated report as a recommended practice of the *King Report of Corporate Governance for South Africa 2009* (King III). Companies listed on the Johannesburg Stock Exchange (JSE) took particular note because the King III principles formed a part of the JSE Listings Requirements. The birth of the integrated report spurred the formation of the Integrated Reporting Committee (IRC) of South Africa.[49] The IRC was established as a national body comprising the major professional and industry bodies with an interest in corporate reporting. Its first task was to develop a discussion paper on a framework for an integrated report to assist listed companies and other organisations.

---

[48] The IRC of SA released an Information Paper on *Preparing an Integrated Report: A Starter's Guide (Updated)* in August 2018 which is a useful reference source for SMMEs and others new to integrated reporting. See www.integratedreportingsa.org.

[49] See www.integratedreportingsa.org.

In January 2011, the IRC released the world's first framework for an integrated report.[50] This framework later fed into the development of the *International <IR> Framework* released by the International Integrated Reporting Council (IIRC) in December 2013. South Africa contributed in other ways too: the experience of its companies was shared, as was the expertise and thinking of a number of South Africans (including the authors of this book) who participated in the working group and project groups involved in the development of the *International <IR> Framework*.

Today, the IRC of South Africa releases technical Information Papers and FAQs to assist companies and organisations with improving their integrated reports. It continues to promote integrated reporting in South Africa and collaborates with other organisations on this. In 2017, the IRC extended its membership base to corporate members.[51]

What happens in integrated reporting in South Africa is noticed by other countries. South African companies have been preparing reports for the longest time and South Africa produces the most reports. It is indeed true to say that, in South Africa, integrated reports are commonplace. Integrated reports are released by JSE-listed companies, large public sector and state-owned organisations, as well as non-profit and professional organisations. However, some sectors need to catch up, namely SMMEs and retirement funds.

In 2016, the King Committee issued the *King Report on Corporate Governance for South Africa 2016* (King IV). King IV similarly recommends the practice of preparing an integrated report each year. King IV was released with five sector supplements to guide governance in the SMME sector, retirement funds, municipalities, public sector organisations and non-profit organisations. Each sector supplement contains the recommended practice of preparing an integrated report.

King IV incorporates the concepts of integrated reporting and integrated thinking and is aligned with the *International <IR> Framework*. The IRC of SA endorsed the *International <IR> Framework* as good practice on how to prepare an integrated report in April 2015. King IV states that the guidance of the IRC of SA on integrated reporting should be followed.

---

[50] See www.integratedreportingsa.org.

[51] To learn more about the IRC and its members, see www.integratedreportingsa.org.

Value creation, preservation or erosion are the effects (outcomes) that the organisation has on the six capitals through its business activities and products and services (page 6).

The six capitals assist organisations in identifying all the resources and relationships it uses and effects for holistic and complete reporting. They are:
1. Financial capital
2. Manufactured capital
3. Intellectual capital
4. Human capital
5. Social and relationship capital
6. Natural capital

Each capital holds inherent benefits, risks and opportunities to the organisation and the capitals are interdependent. Although all six capitals may not be equally significant, an organisation will still consider the effects on the capital in an integrated way (page 4).

The <IR> Framework's
GUIDING PRINCIPLES
assist in determining the information to be reported.
The seven Guiding Principles are:
1. Strategic focus and future orientation
2. Connectivity of information
3. Stakeholder relationships
4. Materiality
5. Conciseness
6. Reliability and completeness
7. Consistency and comparability

(page 11)

The <IR> Framework sets out eight **Content Elements** (these can be seen as information areas):
1. Organisational overview and external environment
2. Governance
3. Business model
4. Risks and opportunities
5. Strategy and resource allocation
6. Performance
7. Outlook
8. Basis of preparation and presentation
(page 12)

There are **19 requirements** to qualify a report as an integrated report prepared in accordance with the <IR> Framework. The 19 requirements include the Guiding Principles and Content Elements (refer to pages 34 and 35 of The <IR> Framework's for the full list).

PLANNING AND PREPARING THE INTEGRATED REPORT

The governing body has ultimate accountability ... (page 16)	It is essential that the organisation's leadership buys into and participates in its integrated report. The governing body owns the report - it gives final approval of the report, and the material matters therein, and oversees its preparation.
The reporting process does not have to be complicated ... (page 14)	There is no one-size-fits-all integrated report or integrated reporting process. The reporting process is scalable and may require effort in proportion to the size and structure of the organisation - the process need not be complicated. However, the need for responsibility and early and thorough planning cannot be emphasised enough. The governing body may designate a senior executive responsible for the preparation of the report.
Determining materiality is one of the cornerstones of an effective report ... (page 21)	Applying materiality means that the organisation reports on all the matters that substantively affect its ability to create value. Material matters cover all aspects of the organisation - strategy, governance, performance, prospects, and the six capitals. The integrated report discloses the process for determining materiality and the governing body approves the process and identified material matters.
Reliable information is important for the integrity and credibility of the report ... (page 17)	Collecting non-financial data and translating it into an accessible format can be challenging at first. In practising integrated reporting, organisations become better at collecting and integrating this data, which can improve their business operations and decision making. The governing body determines the assurance approach for the report which often includes internal and/or external assurance.
Aim to produce a frank and balanced report ...	The integrated report should be transparent, accessible and understandable. A good integrated report is clear, concise, easy to understand and uncluttered by detailed information or information that is not material. The report is the organisation's value creation story; additional and detailed information can be housed in supplementary reports, fact sheets or the website. The integrated report should be balanced and transparent, reflecting both good and poor performance and outcomes. Users have said that unbalanced reporting damages an organisation's credibility.

Figure 8: The information flow and preparation process (the page references refer to sections covered in the *Starter's Guide (updated)*)[52]

---

[52] Integrated Reporting Committee (IRC) of South Africa *Preparing an Integrated Report: A Starter's Guide (Updated)* (August 2018) at www.integratedreportingsa.org.

Chapter 11   The Investment Circle

There is a great irony in the world's immense investment industry. Individuals hand over their savings money to the pension and asset management funds to invest. The funds duly invest this money in the shares and debt instruments of companies around the world. The companies conduct their business and strive for ever-rising financial returns – but many render these returns at the expense of negative effects on society and the environment. This is the same society and environment lived in by the individuals who hand over their savings money to the pension and asset management funds. Why don't individuals take more active interest in where their money is invested?

***

There is a second great irony. It lies in the term 'responsible investment'. Responsible investment focuses on environmental, social and governance (ESG) issues in investee companies and many institutional investors have specific investment funds dedicated to responsible investment. But ESG issues are not separate from the business of any company – they are core to it. They play a pivotal role in determining the financial future of the company, which means they should be considered by all investors in their investment selection and monitoring process and not only by the dedicated responsible investment funds.

***

Times are changing.

The majority of the asset owners (the pension funds) and asset managers in the world have adopted the United Nations Principles of Responsible Investment (UNPRI).[53] The six principles are wrapped around the ESG issues which an organisation faces.

A proposal to stock exchanges for their listings standards to include reporting requirements on ESG issues is being considered by the 60 members of the World Federation of Stock Exchanges. This was developed by asset owners and asset managers and other UNPRI signatories.

---

[53] See https://www.unpri.org/.

Many countries have developed their own stewardship codes based on the UNPRI principles. In the EU there is a directive for listed and large companies to include ESG in their corporate thinking. Many regulators have stipulated that financial institutions, including pension funds, should take account of ESG factors in their decision to invest in a company.

Put all of the above in the broader context that we're living in the century of intangible assets, constrained natural resources, and expanding population growth, and it's clear that the due diligence of an investee company by the trustees of pension funds (as the representative shareholder) and/or the directors of asset management companies has to change.

The trustees of a pension fund and their appointed asset managers that, in the 21st century, invest in the shares of a listed company by merely analysing the financial statements are failing in their duty of care. A study[54] of the S&P 500 index on the New York Stock Exchange shows that just 16 per cent of the market cap is reflected as tangible assets in the balance sheet. The market value of a company can include factors such as patents, copyrights, brand, reputation, supply chain conduct and how it's being monitored, the adequacy of internal controls, a focus on sustainable development, trust and confidence within the community it operates in, legitimacy of operations, and quality governance. The trustees of pension funds and their asset managers have to change their toolbox for the due diligence they carry out on a company before investing their beneficiaries' money.

Their toolbox must incorporate consideration of the ESG issues of a company and of how its board has dealt with these issues. Their toolbox should cover:

- Does the company's **purpose** include positive effects for society and the environment?

- Does the company's **business model and strategy** incorporate the UN's Sustainable Development Goals (SDGs) pertinent to the company's business? For example, a fisheries company might consider SDG 3 on good health and well-being, SDG 12 on responsible production and consumption, SDG 13 on climate action, and SDG 14 on life below water.

- The 21st century must be a century of sustainable development. It has been scientifically established that the 20th century was a century of unsustainable development. The SDGs, paraphrased, effectively state that business is at the

---

[54] Ocean Tomo LLC *Intangible Asset Market Value Study* (2017) at http://www.oceantomo.com/intangible-asset-market-value-study/.

junction of the three critical dimensions of sustainable development: the economy, society and the environment. Consequently, in a due diligence, it must be asked whether a company has a business model which has, or is striving to have, a positive effect on all three. This is critical because a company could be successful financially, but have a business model which is so adverse to the environment that holistically it is destroying value for society. This is certainly not in the long-term best interests of the beneficiaries of a pension fund – rather, they should be invested in a company which has a business model which has a positive effect on their society and their environment.

- Does the company's **strategy** deal with the positive and negative outcomes of the company's product or service? Does it deal with how they are going to eradicate or ameliorate the negative outcomes and enhance the positive outcomes?

- What do you know about the company's **ethics and culture**, and is there a code of conduct?

- What is happening in the **supply chain**? History shows that a company will suffer adversely if it's discovered that human rights are violated in the supply chain.

- What is the quality of **governance**? How well informed is the board? Does it have standing agenda items covering inputs and outcomes, stakeholder relationships, resource allocation plans, and technology governance and cybersecurity? Is it achieving the four governance outcomes of quality governance?

- Does the company have sufficient firewalls to protect its **information systems**? The DNA of any business is its information systems. If the information systems are hacked or interfered with internally or by an external party this could cause the collapse of the company.

- Has the company adopted **integrated thinking** through the consideration and management of the six capitals in its inputs to outcomes process and its strategy? This is important as it indicates whether or not the company will be sustainable in the future.

- Does the company release a quality integrated report each year? Has it been prepared using the best practice guidance of the *International <IR> Framework*? Furthermore, has the integrated report flowed from the board which has a unified collective mind?

- An audit is done on the company's tangible assets in its balance sheet using the financial reporting standards to value the assets. Similarly, the company should be able to state what its **intangible assets** are and what it regards as the value of these assets. If the two values do not equate to the market value, assuming that the company is listed, the reasons for the difference need to be interrogated.

When Luca Pacioli developed the double-entry bookkeeping system in the 15th century he formed the foundation of today's accounting standards. Financial institutions, however, can no longer rely only on the financial statements. The example of Netflix is famously used here. In 2016, the financial statements showed that the company was hundreds of millions of dollars in the red, but this was blithely ignored by investors, who were convinced that the intellectual property of online streaming would result in the eventual destruction of cable TV.

It has to be asked if the trustees of pension funds and their asset managers really understand what is going on in the companies they invest in. Can they really make an informed assessment about the company having a value creation process which will be carried out in a sustainable manner?

Trustees generally need to spend more time truly understanding the financial and non-financial factors of the companies they invest in. They need to take greater care in making investment decisions on behalf of their beneficiaries than they would take if they were dealing with their own family's money. They need to ask themselves the intellectually naïve questions that a non-executive director would ask (see chapter 8).

The board of trustees of the pension fund itself has to have an ethical culture and act with effective leadership. It is critical for them to show that good governance is practised in the fund.

A pension fund, as is the case with similar financial institutions, should develop an investment policy statement which embraces the changed world of the 21st century. This will ensure that it is investing in companies that have a business model and strategy which embeds the sustainability issues core to the business, as well as one that fits into the digital world in which we live. Pension funds and asset managers should be transparently reporting to their beneficiaries through an annual integrated report.

Chapter 12   Making the Change: Seven Steps

1. Having the board on board (chapter 7)

The commitment of the board to focusing on the long-term health of the company is essential. As part of their ongoing training, a workshop session for the directors to be informed about and understand the changes in the external environment and the need for integrated thinking is suggested.

2. Start the integrated reporting process (chapter 10)

Many companies have found that the initiation of the integrated reporting process kick-started the change in mindset and thinking within the company. At the behest of the board, the first thing for management to do is to set up an Integrated Reporting team[55] dedicated to facilitating the preparation of the annual integrated report. The team first gets to grips with understanding the requirements of the *International <IR> Framework*. The *International <IR> Framework* is a beautiful piece of work: it explains the concepts, sets out the Guiding Principles that guide the information suitable for the report, and its Content Elements offer a structure for the report (organisational overview and external environment, governance, business model, strategy and resource allocation plans, risks and opportunities, performance, outlook).[56]

3. The business model (chapter 4)

Drawing up the business model affords a thorough understanding of the reality of the business of the company. Firstly, the business model depicts the resources and relationships that the company depends on (categorised into six types of capital: financial, intellectual, manufactured, human, natural, social and relationships). Secondly, the business model shows the company's outcomes on the six capitals, ie the positive and adverse effects it is having. This is important information to the company. Knowing its inputs and outcomes informs strategy, which is how the company will eradicate or ameliorate adverse outcomes and enhance positive ones. The understanding also informs risks and opportunities

---

[55] An inter-departmental team reporting to the CEO or the CFO.

[56] A useful resource for new reporters is *Preparing an Integrated Report: A Starter's Guide (Updated)* (August 2018) at www.integratedreportingsa.org.

and the company's relationships with its stakeholders. Furthermore, there is awareness that how the company treats its capitals today will influence their future price, quality and availability.

Honesty, rather than denial about adverse effects, and a willingness to look further than the short term are essential in drawing up the business model. It's imperative for the board to discuss and agree on the inputs and the outcomes on the six capitals – and in so doing help it steer clear of a 'media moment' of awareness of adverse effects, as highlighted in chapter 2.

4. The external environment

The company operates in an external environment which is a heaving mass of global and local push and pull influences and shifts in societal thinking. Understanding the major forces, and the future scenarios, informs the company's path ahead. This information informs on strategy, risks and opportunities, governance practices, remuneration, the company's relationships with its stakeholders and the company's outlook.

5. Strategy (chapter 4)

Knowledge of the business model showing the company's inputs and outcomes and its externalities influences strategy. Many boards have found that they had to re-assess their strategy and strategic objectives after this greater awareness.

In considering and approving the reassessed strategy and strategic objectives, the board determines the key performance indicators (KPIs) used to measure achievement and sets the performance targets. The board ensures that these same KPIs are used in the calculation of performance bonuses and share incentives to the CEO and management. After all, why would they focus on financial performance when the business model shows that the company's future is determined by other key factors too?

It's essential that awareness of the strategic objectives is spread throughout the company. Everyone who works for and is a part of the company should know what the company aims to achieve. It's a matter of getting the 'feet on the ground to march in unison to the tune at the top'. In a large company it can result in different departments, for instance, marketing and business development, making more informed and hence better decisions, rather than siloed ones.

Strategy also embraces the company's plans to ensure it has continued access to the inputs it needs to achieve its objectives in the years ahead.

6. Risks and opportunities

Knowledge of the business model facilitates a greater understanding of the risks facing the company, and of the opportunities that lie within those risks.

7. Systems

Systems to get the required information – performance against KPI targets, determination of risks and opportunities, inputs, outcomes, stakeholder feedback – have to be put in place. This information is core to the company and should fall into the regular management review function and process. It should also be included in the information packs to the board for its meetings. The annual information will go into the integrated report. Information systems are the very DNA of a company. The protection of that information is critical. Hence, at every board meeting, there should be an agenda item for information technology and cyber security.

The preparation of the integrated report – and a mindful application of the requirements of the *International <IR> Framework* – is a significant push factor in embedding integrated thinking in the company. And integrated thinking in the company is what you want to achieve for it to be a healthy company.

Chapter 13   The Healthy Company

The company with a purpose, business model and strategy that adds value to society and the environment in a sustainable manner is a healthy one. It is a company that embraces inclusive capitalism.

Throughout the 20th century, with companies' prime focus on increasing shareholder wealth and company profit, adverse outcomes were borne by society and the environment. Society was duly outraged. This, without doubt, has contributed to the low level of trust between companies and stakeholders that persists today. It also contributed to the era of unsustainable development with ecological overshoot (where natural resources were used faster than nature was regenerating them) reached in 1997.

A healthy company has conscious directors who care about the future of their incapacitated charge, the company. Directors are the heart, mind, soul and conscience of the company. If the directors are not conscious leaders, the company will not be seen to be a healthy one.

Conscious leaders are aware of the changed world of the 21st century: they take account of it being natural resource constrained, technologically advanced, but with an increasing population. With fewer natural resources, companies have to produce more but with less. Companies cannot carry on business as usual by merely focusing on financial aspects and increasing shareholder wealth. The suggestion that the wealth created would trickle down to the unequal at the bottom has not happened. The trickle became treacle and it stuck.

The healthy company arises out of the realisation by directors that they are the conscience of the company. They must honestly apply their minds with knowledge of the legitimate and reasonable needs, interests and expectations of stakeholders, and with the purpose of the company embodying more than shareholder gains. Customers, employees and other stakeholders, particularly millennials, require this. Society requires this.

Conscious leaders take account of the six capitals – financial, manufactured, intellectual, human, natural, and social and relationships – in the inputs the company uses and relies on, and ensure that the company strategically deals with the outcomes on these capitals of the company's products or services. They strive to ensure the company's business model and strategy has positive effects on the economy, society and the environment and take action to eradicate or ameliorate any adverse effects. In this way, they participate in the new era of sustainable development.

Conscious leaders ensure the company is practising quality governance in order to be a healthy one. They know the best way is a mindful approach and not a mindless checklist approach. They know the mindful approach is ethical and effective leadership that achieves the four good governance outcomes as suggested in the King IV Code (see chapter 7).

The world has moved away from financial capitalism that focuses solely on shareholder interests and success being defined as increased profit, increased share prices and increased dividends. Today, the success of a company is looked at through a value creation lens: are the outcomes positive for society, the economy and the environment? The asset owners and asset managers of the world, in adopting the UN's Principles of Responsible Investment, are a huge driver of conscious leaders ensuring that the companies they steer are consciously healthy ones. Inclusive capitalism is also a driver of healthy companies.

Conscious leadership leads to an outcome that there is a long-term strategy for the health of the company – rather than the short-term wealth of only one of its stakeholders, its shareholders. If the unified collective mind of the board develops a business model which has positive outcomes, then the company will be a healthy one. Importantly, it will be seen to be a healthy one and a good corporate citizen.

In today's radically transparent world this is of the utmost importance, because civil society has become a bigger disruptor of business today than shareholder activism.

Appendix 1 *International <IR> Framework (2021)*

Reproduced with the kind permission of the International Integrated Reporting Council

INTEGRATED REPORTING <IR>

INTERNATIONAL <IR> FRAMEWORK

JANUARY 2021

About the IIRC

The International Integrated Reporting Council (IIRC) is a global coalition of regulators, investors, companies, standard setters, the accounting profession, academia and NGOs. Together, this coalition shares the view that communication about value creation, preservation or erosion is the next step in the evolution of corporate reporting.

The International <IR> Framework was developed to meet this need and provide a foundation for the future.

> The International <IR> Framework (January 2021) supersedes the International <IR> Framework (December 2013). This latest version applies to reporting periods commencing 1 January 2022. Earlier application is welcome.

Further information about the IIRC can be found on its website www.integratedreporting.org, including its:

- Purpose, mission and vision
- Structure and membership
- Governance and funding
- Procedures Handbook.

Other resources

For more on integrated reporting and how the <IR> Framework can be applied, visit the IIRC's Frequently Asked Questions and <IR> Examples Database.

The IIRC does not accept responsibility for loss caused to any person who acts, or refrains from acting, in reliance on the material in this publication, whether such loss is caused by negligence or otherwise.

Copyright © January 2021 by the International Integrated Reporting Council ('the IIRC'). All rights reserved. Permission is granted to make copies of this work, provided that such copies are for personal or educational use and are not sold or disseminated and provided that each copy bears the following credit line: "Copyright © January 2021 by the International Integrated Reporting Council ('the IIRC'). All rights reserved. Used with permission of the IIRC. Contact the IIRC (info@theiirc.org) for permission to reproduce, store, transmit or make other uses of this document." Otherwise, prior written permission from the IIRC is required to reproduce, store, transmit or make other uses of this document, except as permitted by law. Contact: info@theiirc.org.

About integrated reporting

The IIRC's long-term vision is a world in which <u>integrated thinking</u> is embedded within mainstream business practice in the public and private sectors, facilitated by <u>integrated reporting</u> as the corporate reporting norm. The cycle of integrated reporting and thinking, resulting in efficient and productive capital allocation, will act as a force for financial stability and sustainable development.

Integrated reporting aims to:

- Improve the quality of information available to providers of financial capital to enable a more efficient and productive allocation of capital

- Promote a more cohesive and efficient approach to corporate reporting that draws on different reporting strands and communicates the full range of factors that materially affect the ability of an organization to create value over time

- Enhance accountability and stewardship for the broad base of capitals (financial, manufactured, intellectual, human, social and relationship, and natural) and promote understanding of their interdependencies

- Support integrated thinking, decision-making and actions that focus on the creation of value over the short, medium and long term.

Integrated reporting is consistent with numerous developments in corporate reporting taking place within national jurisdictions across the world. It is intended that the <IR> Framework, which provides principles-based guidance for companies and other organizations wishing to prepare an integrated report, will accelerate these individual initiatives and provide impetus to greater innovation in corporate reporting globally to unlock the benefits of integrated reporting, including the increased efficiency of the reporting process itself.

It is anticipated that, over time, integrated reporting will become the corporate reporting norm. No longer will an organization produce numerous, disconnected and static communications. This will be delivered by the process of integrated thinking and the application of principles such as connectivity of information.

Integrated reporting is part of an evolving corporate reporting system. This system is enabled by comprehensive frameworks and standards, addressing measurement and disclosure in relation to all capitals, appropriate regulation and effective assurance. Integrated reporting is consistent with developments in financial and other reporting, but an integrated report also differs from other reports and communications in a number of ways. In particular, it focuses on the ability of an organization to create value in the short, medium and long term, and in so doing it:

- Has a combined emphasis on conciseness, strategic focus and future orientation, the connectivity of information and the capitals and their interdependencies

- Emphasizes the importance of integrated thinking within the organization.

Integrated thinking is the active consideration by an organization of the relationships between its various operating and functional units and the capitals that the organization uses or affects. Integrated thinking leads to integrated decision-making and actions that consider the creation, preservation or erosion of value over the short, medium and long term.

Integrated thinking takes into account the connectivity and interdependencies between the range of factors that affect an organization's ability to create value over time, including:

- The capitals that the organization uses or affects, and the critical interdependencies, including trade-offs, between them

- The capacity of the organization to respond to key stakeholders' legitimate needs and interests

- How the organization tailors its business model and strategy to respond to its external environment and the risks and opportunities it faces

- The organization's activities, performance (financial and other) and outcomes in terms of the capitals – past, present and future.

The more that integrated thinking is embedded into an organization's activities, the more naturally will the connectivity of information flow into management reporting, analysis and decision-making. It also leads to better integration of the information systems that support internal and external reporting and communication, including preparation of the integrated report.

CONTENTS

EXECUTIVE SUMMARY

Integrated reporting promotes a more cohesive and efficient approach to corporate reporting and aims to improve the quality of information available to providers of financial capital to enable a more efficient and productive allocation of capital.

The IIRC's long-term vision is a world in which integrated thinking is embedded within mainstream business practice in the public and private sectors, facilitated by integrated reporting as the corporate reporting norm.

An Integrated Report

The primary purpose of an integrated report is to explain to providers of financial capital how an organization creates, preserves or erodes value over time. An integrated report benefits all stakeholders interested in an organization's ability to create value over time, including employees, customers, suppliers, business partners, local communities, legislators, regulators and policy-makers.

The <IR> Framework takes a principles-based approach. The intent is to strike an appropriate balance between flexibility and prescription that recognizes the wide variation in individual circumstances of different organizations while enabling a sufficient degree of comparability across organizations to meet relevant information needs. It does not prescribe specific key performance indicators, measurement methods, or the disclosure of individual matters, but does include a small number of requirements that are to be applied before an integrated report can be said to be in accordance with the <IR> Framework.

An integrated report may be prepared in response to existing compliance requirements, and may be either a standalone report or be included as a distinguishable, prominent and accessible part of another report or communication. It should include a statement by those charged with governance accepting responsibility for the report.

Fundamental Concepts

An integrated report aims to provide insight about the resources and relationships used and affected by an organization – these are collectively referred to as "the capitals" in the <IR> Framework. It also seeks to explain how the organization interacts with the external environment and the capitals to create, preserve or erode value over the short, medium and long term.

The capitals are stocks of value that are increased, decreased or transformed through the activities and outputs of the organization. They are categorized in the <IR> Framework as financial, manufactured, intellectual, human, social and relationship, and natural capital, although organizations preparing an integrated report are not required to adopt this categorization or to structure their report along the lines of the capitals.

The ability of an organization to create value for itself enables financial returns to the providers of financial capital. This is interrelated with the value the organization creates for stakeholders and society at large through a wide range of activities, interactions and relationships. When these are material to the organization's ability to create value for itself, they are included in the integrated report.

The <IR> Framework

The purpose of the <IR> Framework is to establish Guiding Principles and Content Elements that govern the overall content of an integrated report, and to explain the fundamental concepts that underpin them. The <IR> Framework:

- Identifies information to be included in an integrated report for use in assessing the organization's ability to create value; it does not set benchmarks for such things as the quality of an organization's strategy or the level of its performance

- Is written primarily in the context of private sector, for-profit companies of any size but it can also be applied, adapted as necessary, by public sector and not-for-profit organizations.

Guiding Principles

Seven Guiding Principles underpin the preparation and presentation of an integrated report, informing the content of the report and how information is presented:

- *Strategic focus and future orientation.* An integrated report should provide insight into the organization's strategy, and how it relates to the organization's ability to create value in the short, medium and long term, and to its use of and effects on the capitals

- *Connectivity of information.* An integrated report should show a holistic picture of the combination, interrelatedness and dependencies between the factors that affect the organization's ability to create value over time

- *Stakeholder relationships.* An integrated report should provide insight into the nature and quality of the organization's relationships with its key stakeholders, including how and to what extent the organization understands, takes into account and responds to their legitimate needs and interests

- *Materiality.* An integrated report should disclose information about matters that substantively affect the organization's ability to create value over the short, medium and long term

- *Conciseness.* An integrated report should be concise

- *Reliability and completeness.* An integrated report should include all material matters, both positive and negative, in a balanced way and without material error

- *Consistency and comparability.* The information in an integrated report should be presented: (a) on a basis that is consistent over time; and (b) in a way that enables comparison with other organizations to the extent it is material to the organization's own ability to create value over time.

Content Elements

An integrated report includes eight Content Elements that are fundamentally linked to each other and are not mutually exclusive:

- *Organizational overview and external environment.* What does the organization do and what are the circumstances under which it operates?

- *Governance.* How does the organization's governance structure support its ability to create value in the short, medium and long term?

- *Business model.* What is the organization's business model?

- *Risks and opportunities.* What are the specific risks and opportunities that affect the organization's ability to create value over the short, medium and long term, and how is the organization dealing with them?

- *Strategy and resource allocation.* Where does the organization want to go and how does it intend to get there?

- *Performance.* To what extent has the organization achieved its strategic objectives for the period and what are its outcomes in terms of effects on the capitals?

- *Outlook.* What challenges and uncertainties is the organization likely to encounter in pursuing its strategy, and what are the potential implications or its business model and future performance?

- *Basis of presentation.* How does the organization determine what matters to include in the integrated report and how are such matters quantified or evaluated?

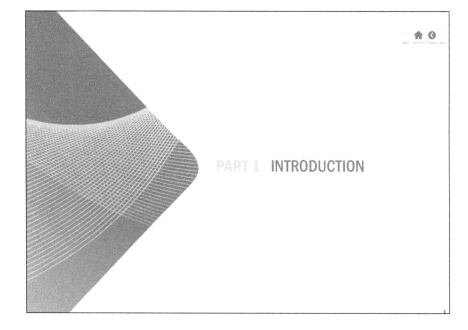

PART 1 INTRODUCTION

1. Using the <IR> Framework

1A Integrated report defined

1.1 An integrated report is a concise communication about how an organization's strategy, governance, performance and prospects, in the context of its external environment, lead to the creation, preservation or erosion of value over the short, medium and long term.

1.2 An integrated report should be prepared in accordance with the <IR> Framework.

1B Objective of the <IR> Framework

1.3 The purpose of the <IR> Framework is to establish Guiding Principles and Content Elements that govern the overall content of an integrated report, and to explain the fundamental concepts that underpin them.

1.4 The <IR> Framework is written primarily in the context of private sector, for-profit companies of any size but it can also be applied, adapted as necessary, by public sector and not-for-profit organizations.

1.5 The <IR> Framework identifies information to be included in an integrated report for use in assessing an organization's ability to create value; it does not set benchmarks for such things as the quality of an organization's strategy or the level of its performance.

1.6 In the <IR> Framework, reference to the creation of value:

* Includes instances when value is preserved and when it is eroded (see paragraph 2.14)

* Relates to value creation over time (i.e. over the short, medium and long term).

1C Purpose and users of an integrated report

1.7 The primary purpose of an integrated report is to explain to providers of financial capital how an organization creates, preserves or erodes value over time. It therefore contains relevant information, both financial and other.

1.8 An integrated report benefits all stakeholders interested in an organization's ability to create value over time, including employees, customers, suppliers, business partners, local communities, legislators, regulators and policy-makers.

1D A principles-based approach

1.9 The <IR> Framework is principles-based. The intent of the principles-based approach is to strike an appropriate balance between flexibility and prescription that recognizes the wide variation in individual circumstances of different organizations while enabling a sufficient degree of comparability across organizations to meet relevant information needs.

1.10 The <IR> Framework does not prescribe specific key performance indicators, measurement methods or the disclosure of individual matters. Those responsible for the preparation and presentation of the integrated report therefore need to exercise judgement, given the specific circumstances of the organization, to determine:

* Which matters are material

* How they are disclosed, including the application of generally accepted measurement and disclosure methods as appropriate. When information in an integrated report is similar to, or based on other information published by the organization, it is prepared on the same basis as, or is easily reconcilable with, that other information.

Quantitative and qualitative information

1.11 Quantitative indicators, including key performance indicators and monetized metrics, and the context in which they are provided can be very helpful in explaining how an organization creates, preserves or erodes value and how it uses and affects various capitals. While quantitative indicators are included in an integrated report whenever it is practicable and relevant to do so:

- The ability of the organization to create value can best be reported on through a combination of quantitative and qualitative information. (See also paragraph 3.8 regarding the connectivity of quantitative and qualitative information.)

- It is not the purpose of an integrated report to quantify or monetize the value of the organization at a point in time, the value it creates, preserves or erodes over a period, or its uses of or effects on all the capitals. (See also paragraph 5.5 for common characteristics of suitable quantitative indicators.)

1E Form of report and relationship with other information

1.12 An integrated report should be a designated, identifiable communication.

1.13 An integrated report is intended to be more than a summary of information in other communications (e.g. financial statements, a sustainability report, analyst calls, or on a website); rather, it makes explicit the connectivity of information to communicate how value is created, preserved or eroded over time.

1.14 An integrated report may be prepared in response to existing compliance requirements. For example, an organization may be required by local law to prepare a management commentary or other report that provides context for its financial statements. If that report is also prepared in accordance with the <IR> Framework it can be considered an integrated report. If the report is required to include specified information beyond that required by the <IR> Framework, the report can still be considered an

integrated report if that other information does not obscure the concise information required by the <IR> Framework.

1.15 An integrated report may be either a standalone report or be included as a distinguishable, prominent and accessible part of another report or communication. For example, it may be included at the front of a report that also includes the organization's financial statements.

1.16 An integrated report can provide an "entry point" to more detailed information outside the designated communication, to which it may be linked. The form of link will depend on the form of the integrated report (e.g. for a paper-based report, links may involve attaching other information as an appendix; for a web-based report, it may involve hyperlinking to that other information).

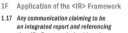

1F Application of the <IR> Framework

1.17 Any communication claiming to be an integrated report and referencing the <IR> Framework should apply all the requirements identified in bold italic type unless:

- **The unavailability of reliable information or specific legal prohibitions results in an inability to disclose material information**

- **Disclosure of material information would cause significant competitive harm. (See paragraph 3.51.)**

1.18 In the case of the unavailability of reliable information or specific legal prohibitions, an integrated report should:

- **Indicate the nature of the information that has been omitted**

- **Explain the reason why it has been omitted**

- **In the case of the unavailability of data, identify the steps being taken to obtain the information and the expected time frame for doing so.**

Guidance

1.19 Text in the <IR> Framework that is not in bold italic type provides guidance to assist in applying the requirements. It is not necessary for an integrated report to include all matters referred to in the guidance.

1G Responsibility for an integrated report

1.20 *An integrated report should include a statement from those charged with governance that includes:*

- *An acknowledgement of their responsibility to ensure the integrity of the integrated report*

- *Their opinion or conclusion about whether, or the extent to which, the integrated report is presented in accordance with the <IR> Framework.*

Where legal or regulatory requirements preclude a statement of responsibility from those charged with governance, this should be clearly stated.

1.21 The extent to which the integrated report is presented in accordance with the <IR> Framework is evaluated against the requirements identified in bold italic type and summarized in the Appendix.

Where an organization is in the process of adopting the <IR> Framework, it is appropriate to identify which requirements have not been applied and the reasons why.

1.22 In applying paragraph **1.20**, the organization will take into account its own governance structure, which is a function of its jurisdiction, cultural and legal context, size and ownership characteristics. For example, some jurisdictions require a single-tier board, while others require the separation of supervisory and executive/management functions within a two-tier board. In the case of two-tier boards, the statement of responsibility is ordinarily provided by the body responsible for overseeing the strategic direction of the organization.

It is important to consider the intent of paragraph **1.20**, which is to promote the integrity of the integrated report through the commitment of the body responsible for overseeing the strategic direction of the organization.

1.23 In cases where legal or regulatory requirements preclude a statement of responsibility from those charged with governance, an explanation of measures taken to ensure the integrity of the integrated report can provide important insight to users. Accordingly, disclosures about the process followed to prepare and present the integrated report are encouraged. Such disclosures can include:

- Related systems, procedures and controls, including key responsibilities and activities

- The role of those charged with governance, including relevant committees.

1.24 Process disclosures are encouraged as a supplement to a statement of responsibility from those charged with governance as this information indicates measures taken to ensure the integrity of the integrated report.

---

2. Fundamental Concepts

2.1 The Fundamental Concepts underpin and reinforce the requirements and guidance in the <IR> Framework.

2A Introduction

2.2 An integrated report explains how an organization creates, preserves or erodes value over time. Value is not created, preserved or eroded by or within an organization alone. It is:

- Influenced by the external environment

- Created through relationships with stakeholders

- Dependent on various resources.

2.3 An integrated report therefore aims to provide insight about:

- The external environment that affects an organization

- The resources and the relationships used and affected by the organization, which are referred to collectively in the <IR> Framework as the capitals and are categorized in Section 2C as financial, manufactured, intellectual, human, social and relationship, and natural

- How the organization interacts with the external environment and the capitals to create, preserve or erode value over the short, medium and long term.

2B   Value creation, preservation or erosion for the organization and for others

2.4   Value created, preserved or eroded by an organization over time manifests itself in increases, decreases or transformations of the capitals caused by the organization's business activities and outputs. That value has two interrelated aspects – value created, preserved or eroded for:

* The organization itself, which affects financial returns to the providers of financial capital

* Others (i.e. stakeholders and society at large).

2.5   Providers of financial capital are interested in the value an organization creates for itself. They are also interested in the value an organization creates for others when it affects the ability of the organization to create value for itself, or relates to a stated objective of the organization (e.g. an explicit social purpose) that affects their assessments.

2.6   The ability of an organization to create value for itself is linked to the value it creates for others. As illustrated in Figure 1, this happens through a wide range of activities, interactions and relationships in addition to those, such as sales to customers, that are directly associated with changes in financial capital. These include, for example, the effects of the organization's business activities and outputs on customer satisfaction, suppliers' willingness to trade with the organization and the terms and conditions upon which they do so, the initiatives that business partners agree to undertake with the organization, the organization's reputation, conditions imposed on the organization's social licence to operate, and the imposition of supply chain conditions or legal requirements.

2.7   When these interactions, activities, and relationships are material to the organization's ability to create value for itself, they are included in the integrated report.

This includes taking account of the extent to which effects on the capitals have been externalized (i.e. the costs or other effects on capitals that are not owned by the organization).

Figure 1. Value created, preserved or eroded for the organization and for others

---

2.8   Externalities may be positive or negative (i.e. they may result in a net increase or decrease to the value embodied in the capitals). Externalities may ultimately increase or decrease value created for the organization; therefore, providers of financial capital need information about material externalities to assess their effects and allocate resources accordingly.

2.9   Because value is created over different time horizons and for different stakeholders through different capitals, it is unlikely to be created through the maximization of one capital while disregarding the others. For example, the maximization of financial capital (e.g. profit) at the expense of human capital (e.g. through inappropriate human resource policies and practices) is unlikely to maximize value for the organization in the longer term.

2C The capitals

The stock and flow of capitals

2.10 All organizations depend on various forms of capital for their success. In the <IR> Framework, the capitals comprise financial, manufactured, intellectual, human, social and relationship, and natural, although as discussed in paragraphs 2.17-2.19, organizations preparing an integrated report are not required to adopt this categorization.

2.11 The capitals are stocks of value that are increased, decreased or transformed through the activities and outputs of the organization. For example, an organization's financial capital is increased when it makes a profit, and the quality of its human capital is improved when employees become better trained.

2.12 The overall stock of capitals is not fixed over time. There is a constant flow between and within the capitals as they are increased, decreased or transformed. For example, when an organization improves its human capital through employee training, the related training costs reduce its financial capital. The effect is that financial capital has been transformed into human capital.

Although this example is simple and presented only from the organization's perspective[1], it demonstrates the continuous interaction and transformation between the capitals, albeit with varying rates and outcomes.

2.13 Many activities cause increases, decreases or transformations that are far more complex than the above example and involve a broader mix of capitals or of components within a capital (e.g. the use of water to grow crops that are fed to farm animals, all of which are components of natural capital).

2.14 Although organizations aim to create value overall, this can involve the erosion of value stored in some capitals, resulting in a net decrease to the overall stock of capitals (i.e. value is eroded). In many cases, whether the net effect is an increase or decrease (or neither, i.e. when value is preserved) will depend on the perspective chosen; as in the above example, employees and employers might value training differently.

Categories and descriptions of the capitals

2.15 For the purpose of the <IR> Framework, the capitals are categorized and described on the following page.

---

1 Other perspectives include the increase to the trainer's financial capital due to the payment received from the employer, and the increase to social capital that may occur if employees use newly acquired skills to contribute to community organizations. (See also paragraph 5.6 regarding complexity, interdependencies and trade-offs.)

- *Financial capital* – The pool of funds that is:
  - Available to an organization for use in the production of goods or the provision of services
  - Obtained through financing, such as debt, equity or grants, or generated through operations or investments.

- *Manufactured capital* – Manufactured physical objects (as distinct from natural physical objects) that are available to an organization for use in the production of goods or the provision of services, including:
  - Buildings
  - Equipment
  - Infrastructure (such as roads, ports, bridges, and waste and water treatment plants).

  Manufactured capital is often created by other organizations, but includes assets manufactured by the reporting organization for sale or when they are retained for its own use.

- *Intellectual capital* – Organizational, knowledge-based intangibles, including:
  - Intellectual property, such as patents, copyrights, software, rights and licences
  - "Organizational capital" such as tacit knowledge, systems, procedures and protocols.

- *Human capital* – People's competencies, capabilities and experience, and their motivations to innovate, including their:
  - Alignment with and support for an organization's governance framework, risk management approach, and ethical values
  - Ability to understand, develop and implement an organization's strategy
  - Loyalties and motivations for improving processes, goods and services, including their ability to lead, manage and collaborate.

- *Social and relationship capital* – The institutions and the relationships within and between communities, groups of stakeholders and other networks, and the ability to share information to enhance individual and collective well-being.

  Social and relationship capital includes:
  - Shared norms, and common values and behaviours
  - Key stakeholder relationships, and the trust and willingness to engage that an organization has developed and strives to build and protect with external stakeholders
  - Intangibles associated with the brand and reputation that an organization has developed
  - An organization's social licence to operate.

- *Natural capital* – All renewable and non-renewable environmental resources and processes that provide goods or services that support the past, current or future prosperity of an organization. It includes:
  - Air, water, land, minerals and forests
  - Biodiversity and eco-system health.

2.16 Not all capitals are equally relevant or applicable to all organizations. While most organizations interact with all capitals to some extent, these interactions might be relatively minor or so indirect that they are not sufficiently important to include in the integrated report.

Role of the capitals in the <IR> Framework

2.17 The <IR> Framework does not require an integrated report to adopt the categories identified above or to be structured along the lines of the capitals. Rather, the primary reasons for including the capitals in the <IR> Framework are to serve:

- As part of the theoretical underpinning for the concept of value creation, preservation or erosion (see Section 2B)

- As a guideline for ensuring organizations consider all the forms of capital they use or affect.

2.18 Organizations may categorize the capitals differently. For example, relationships with external stakeholders and the intangibles associated with brand and reputation (both identified as part of social and relationship capital in paragraph 2.15), might be considered by some organizations to be separate capitals, part of other capitals or cutting across a number of individual capitals. Similarly, some organizations define intellectual capital as comprising what they identify as human, "structural" and "relational" capitals.

2.19 Regardless of how an organization categorizes the capitals for its own purposes, the categories identified in paragraph 2.15 are to be used as a guideline to ensure the organization does not overlook a capital that it uses or affects.

2D   Process through which value is created, preserved or eroded

2.20 As noted in paragraph 2.14, although organizations aim to create value, the overall stock of capitals can also either undergo a net decrease or experience no net change. In such cases, value is eroded or preserved. The process through which value is created, preserved or eroded is depicted in Figure 2. It is explained briefly in the following paragraphs, which also identify how the components of Figure 2 (emphasized in bold text) align with the Content Elements in Chapter 4.

2.21 The **external environment**, including economic conditions, technological change, societal issues and environmental challenges, sets the context within which the organization operates. The **purpose, mission and vision** encompass the whole organization, identifying its intention in clear, concise terms. (See Content Element 4A Organizational overview and external environment.)

2.22 Those charged with **governance** are responsible for creating an appropriate oversight structure to support the ability of the organization to create value. (See Content Element 4B Governance.)

2.23 At the core of the organization is its business model, which draws on various capitals as inputs and, through its business activities, converts them to outputs (products, services, by-products and waste). The organization's business activities and outputs lead to outcomes in terms of effects on the capitals. The capacity of the business model to adapt to changes (e.g. in the availability, quality and affordability of inputs) can affect the organization's longer-term viability. (See Content Element 4C Business model.)

2.24 Business activities include the planning, design and manufacture of products or the deployment of specialized skills and knowledge in the provision of services. Encouraging a culture of innovation is often a key business activity in terms of generating new products and services that anticipate customer demand, introducing efficiencies and better use of technology, substituting inputs to minimize adverse social or environmental effects, and finding alternative uses for outputs.

2.25 Outcomes are the internal and external consequences (positive and negative) for the capitals as a result of an organization's business activities and outputs.

2.26 Continuous monitoring and analysis of the external environment in the context of the organization's purpose, mission and vision identifies **risks and opportunities** relevant to the organization, its strategy and its business model. (See Content Element 4D Risks and opportunities.)

Figure 2.Process through which value is created, preserved or eroded

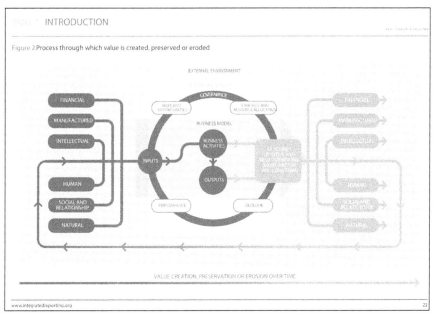

2.27 The organization's **strategy** identifies how it intends to mitigate or manage risks and maximize opportunities. It sets out strategic objectives and strategies to achieve them, which are implemented through **resource allocation** plans. (See Content Element 4E Strategy and resource allocation.)

2.28 The organization needs information about its **performance**, which involves setting up measurement and monitoring systems to provide information for decision-making. (See Content Element 4F Performance.)

2.29 The value creation, preservation or erosion process is not static; regular review of each component and its interactions with other components, and a focus on the organization's **outlook**, lead to revision and refinement to improve all the components. (See Content Element 4G Outlook.)

24

3. Guiding Principles

3.1   The seven Guiding Principles underpin the preparation and presentation of an integrated report, informing the content of the report and how information is presented.

A   Strategic focus and future orientation

B   Connectivity of information

C   Stakeholder relationships

D   Materiality

E   Conciseness

F   Reliability and completeness

G   Consistency and comparability

3.2   These Guiding Principles are applied individually and collectively for the purpose of preparing and presenting an integrated report; accordingly, judgement is needed in applying them, particularly when there is an apparent tension between them (e.g. between conciseness and completeness).

3A   **Strategic focus and future orientation**

3.3   *An integrated report should provide insight into the organization's strategy, and how it relates to the organization's ability to create value in the short, medium and long term and to its use of and effects on the capitals.*

3.4   Applying this Guiding Principle is not limited to the Content Elements 4E Strategy and resource allocation and 4G Outlook. It guides the selection and presentation of other content, and may include, for example:

- Highlighting significant risks, opportunities and dependencies flowing from the organization's market position and business model

- The views of those charged with governance about:
  - The relationship between past and future performance, and the factors that can change that relationship
  - How the organization balances short-, medium- and long-term interests
  - How the organization has learned from past experiences in determining future strategic directions.

3.5 Adopting a strategic focus and future orientation (see also paragraphs 3.52-3.53) includes clearly articulating how the continued availability, quality and affordability of significant capitals contribute to the organization's ability to achieve its strategic objectives in the future and create value.

3B Connectivity of information

3.6 *An integrated report should show a holistic picture of the combination, interrelatedness and dependencies between the factors that affect the organization's ability to create value over time.*

3.7 The more that integrated thinking is embedded into an organization's activities, the more naturally will the connectivity of information flow into management reporting, analysis and decision-making, and subsequently into the integrated report.

3.8 The key forms of connectivity of information include the connectivity between:

- *The Content Elements.* The integrated report connects the Content Elements into a total picture that reflects the dynamic and systemic interactions of the organization's activities as a whole. For example:
  - An analysis of existing resource allocation, and how the organization will combine resources or make further investment to achieve its targeted performance
  - Information about how the organization's strategy is tailored when, for instance, new risks and opportunities are identified or past performance is not as expected

---

- Linking the organization's strategy and business model with changes in its external environment, such as increases or decreases in the pace of technological change, evolving societal expectations, and resource shortages as planetary limits are approached.

- *The past, present and future.* An analysis by the organization of its activities in the past-to-present period can provide useful information to assess the plausibility of what has been reported concerning the present-to-future period. The explanation of the past-to-present period can also be useful in analyzing current capabilities and the quality of management.

- *The capitals.* This includes the interdependencies and trade-offs between the capitals, and how changes in their availability, quality and affordability affect the ability of the organization to create value.

- *Financial and other information.* For example, the implications for:
  - Expected revenue growth or market share of research and development policies, technology/know-how or investment in human resources
  - Cost reduction or new business opportunities of environmental policies, energy efficiency, cooperation with local communities or technologies to tackle social issues
  - Revenue and profit growth of long-term customer relationships, customer satisfaction or reputation.

- *Quantitative and qualitative information.* Both qualitative and quantitative information are necessary for an integrated report to properly represent the organization's ability to create value as each provides context for the other. Including key performance indicators as part of a narrative explanation can be an effective way to connect quantitative and qualitative information.

- *Management information, board information and information reported externally.* For example, as noted in paragraph 5.5, it is important for the quantitative indicators in an integrated report to be consistent with the indicators used internally by management and those charged with governance.

- *Information in the integrated report, information in the organization's other communications, and information from other sources.* This recognizes that all communications from the organization need to be consistent, and that information the organization provides is not read in isolation but combined with information from other sources when making assessments.

3.9 The connectivity of information and the overall usefulness of an integrated report is enhanced when it is logically structured, well presented, written in clear, understandable and jargon-free language, and includes effective navigation devices, such as clearly delineated (but linked) sections and cross-referencing. In this context, information and communication technology can be used to improve the ability to search, access, combine, connect, customize, re-use or analyze information.

3C   Stakeholder relationships

3.10   *An integrated report should provide insight into the nature and quality of the organization's relationships with its key stakeholders, including how and to what extent the organization understands, takes into account and responds to their legitimate needs and interests.*

3.11 This Guiding Principle reflects the importance of relationships with key stakeholders because, as noted in paragraph 2.2, value is not created by or within an organization alone, but is created through relationships with others. It does not mean that an integrated report should attempt to satisfy the information needs of all stakeholders.

3.12 Stakeholders provide useful insights about matters that are important to them, including economic, environmental and social issues that also affect the ability of the organization to create value. These insights can assist the organization to:

* Understand how stakeholders perceive value

* Identify trends that might not yet have come to general attention, but which are rising in significance

* Identify material matters, including risks and opportunities

* Develop and evaluate strategy

* Manage risks

* Implement activities, including strategic and accountable responses to material matters.

3.13 Engagement with stakeholders occurs regularly in the ordinary course of business (e.g. day-to-day liaison with customers and suppliers or broader ongoing engagement as part of strategic planning and risk assessment). It might also be undertaken for a particular purpose (e.g. engagement with a local community when planning a factory extension). The more integrated thinking is embedded in the business, the more likely it is that a fuller consideration of key stakeholders' legitimate needs and interests is incorporated as an ordinary part of conducting business.

3.14 An integrated report enhances transparency and accountability, which are essential in building trust and resilience, by disclosing how key stakeholders' legitimate needs and interests are understood, taken into account and responded to through decisions, actions and performance, as well as ongoing communication.

3.15 Accountability is closely associated with the concept of stewardship and the responsibility of an organization to care for, or use responsibly, the capitals that its activities and outputs affect. When the capitals are owned by the organization, a stewardship responsibility is imposed on management and those charged with governance via their legal responsibilities to the organization.

3.16 When the capitals are owned by others or not owned at all, stewardship responsibilities may be imposed by law or regulation (e.g. through a contract with the owners, or through labour laws or environmental protection regulations). When there is no legal stewardship responsibility, the organization may have an ethical responsibility to accept, or choose to accept stewardship responsibilities and be guided in doing so by stakeholder expectations.

3D   Materiality

3.17   *An integrated report should disclose information about matters that substantively affect the organization's ability to create value over the short, medium and long term.*

The materiality determination process

3.18 The materiality determination process for the purpose of preparing and presenting an integrated report involves:

* Identifying relevant matters based on their ability to affect value creation as discussed in Section 2B (see paragraphs 3.21–3.23)

* Evaluating the importance of relevant matters in terms of their known or potential effect on value creation (see paragraphs 3.24–3.27)

* Prioritizing the matters based on their relative importance (see paragraph 3.28)

* Determining the information to disclose about material matters (see paragraph 3.29).

3.19 This process applies to both positive and negative matters, including risks and opportunities and favourable and unfavourable performance or prospects. It also applies to both financial and other information. Such matters may have direct implications for the organization itself or may affect the capitals owned by or available to others.

3.20 To be most effective, the materiality determination process is integrated into the organization's management processes and includes regular engagement with providers of financial capital and others to ensure the integrated report meets its primary purpose as noted in paragraph 1.7.

Identifying relevant matters

3.21 Relevant matters are those that have, or may have, an effect on the organization's ability to create value. This is determined by considering their effect on the organization's strategy, governance, performance or prospects.

3.22 Ordinarily, matters related to value creation, preservation or erosion that are discussed at meetings of those charged with governance are considered relevant. An understanding of the perspectives of key stakeholders is critical to identifying relevant matters.

3.23 Matters that might be relatively easy to address in the short term but which may, if left unchecked, become more damaging or difficult to address in the medium or long term need to be included in the population of relevant matters. Matters are not excluded on the basis that the organization does not wish to address them or does not know how to deal with them.

Evaluating importance

3.24 Not all relevant matters will be considered material. To be included in an integrated report, a matter also needs to be sufficiently important in terms of its known or potential effect on value creation. This involves evaluating the magnitude of the matter's effect and, if it is uncertain whether the matter will occur, its likelihood of occurrence.

3.25 Magnitude is evaluated by considering whether the matter's effect on strategy, governance, performance or prospects is such that it has the potential to substantively influence value creation, preservation or erosion over time. This requires judgement and will depend on the nature of the matter in question. Matters may be considered material either individually or in the aggregate.

3.26 Evaluating the magnitude of a matter's effect does not imply that the effect needs to be quantified. Depending on the nature of the matter, a qualitative evaluation might be more appropriate.

3.27 In evaluating the magnitude of effect, the organization considers:

- Quantitative and qualitative factors
- Financial, operational, strategic, reputational and regulatory perspectives
- Area of the effect, be it internal or external
- Time frame.

Prioritizing important matters

3.28 Once the population of important matters is identified, they are prioritized based on their magnitude. This helps to focus on the most important matters when determining how they are reported.

Determining information to disclose

3.29 Judgement is applied in determining the information to disclose about material matters. This requires consideration from different perspectives, both internal and external, and is assisted by regular engagement with providers of financial capital and others to ensure the integrated report meets its primary purpose as noted in paragraph 1.7. (See also paragraphs 5.2–5.4.)

Reporting boundary

3.30 Key to the materiality determination process is the concept of the reporting boundary. Determining the boundary for an integrated report has two aspects:

- The financial reporting entity (i.e. the boundary used for financial reporting purposes)
- Risks, opportunities and outcomes attributable to or associated with other entities/stakeholders beyond the financial reporting entity that have a significant effect on the ability of the financial reporting entity to create value.

3.31 The financial reporting entity is central to the reporting boundary because:

- It is the financial reporting entity in which providers of financial capital invest and therefore need information about
- Using the financial reporting entity enables the information in the financial statements to serve as an anchor or point of reference to which the other information in an integrated report can be related.

3.32 Figure 3 depicts the entities/ stakeholders that are considered in determining the reporting boundary.

Figure 3 Entities/stakeholders considered in determining the reporting boundary

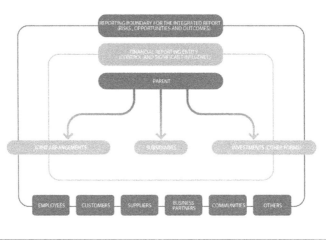

Financial reporting entity

3.33 The financial reporting entity identifies which subsidiaries', joint ventures' and associates' transactions and related events are included in the organization's financial report. The financial reporting entity is determined according to applicable financial reporting standards which revolve around the concepts of control or significant influence.

Risks, opportunities and outcomes

3.34 The second aspect of determining the reporting boundary is to identify those risks, opportunities and outcomes attributable to or associated with entities/stakeholders beyond the financial reporting entity that have a significant effect on the ability of the financial reporting entity to create value. These other entities/stakeholders might be "related parties" for the purpose of financial reporting, but will ordinarily extend further.

3.35 The purpose of looking beyond the financial reporting boundary is to identify risks, opportunities and outcomes that materially affect the organization's ability to create value. The entities/stakeholders within this portion of the reporting boundary are not related to the financial reporting entity by virtue of control or significant influence, but rather by the nature and proximity of the risks, opportunities and outcomes. For example, if aspects of the labour practices in the organization's industry are material to the ability of the organization to create value, then disclosure in the integrated report might include information about those aspects as they relate to suppliers' labour practices.

3E Conciseness

3.36 An integrated report should be concise.

3.37 An integrated report includes sufficient context to understand the organization's strategy, governance, performance and prospects without being burdened with less relevant information.

3.38 The organization seeks a balance in its integrated report between conciseness and the other Guiding Principles, in particular completeness and comparability. In achieving conciseness, an integrated report:

- Applies the materiality determination process described in Section 3D

- Follows a logical structure and includes internal cross-references as appropriate to limit repetition

- May link to more detailed information, information that does not change frequently (e.g. a listing of subsidiaries), or external sources (e.g. assumptions about future economic conditions on a government website)

- Expresses concepts clearly and in as few words as possible

- Favours plain language over the use of jargon or highly technical terminology

- Avoids highly generic disclosures, often referred to as "boilerplate", that are not specific to the organization.

3F   Reliability and completeness

3.39   *An integrated report should include all material matters, both positive and negative, in a balanced way and without material error.*

Reliability

3.40   The reliability of information is affected by its balance and freedom from material error. Reliability (which is often referred to as faithful representation) is enhanced by mechanisms such as robust internal control and reporting systems, stakeholder engagement, internal audit or similar functions, and independent, external assurance.

3.41   Those charged with governance have ultimate responsibility for how the organization's strategy, governance, performance and prospects lead to value creation over time. They are responsible for ensuring that there is effective leadership and decision-making regarding the preparation and presentation of an integrated report, including the identification and oversight of the employees actively involved in the process.

3.42   Maintaining an audit trail when preparing an integrated report helps senior management and those charged with governance review the report and exercise judgement in deciding whether information is sufficiently reliable to be included. It might be appropriate in some cases (e.g. with respect to future-oriented information) for an integrated report to describe the mechanisms employed to ensure reliability.

3.43   Paragraph 1.18 identifies relevant disclosures when material information is omitted because of the unavailability of reliable data.

Balance

3.44   A balanced integrated report has no bias in the selection or presentation of information. Information in the report is not slanted, weighted, emphasized, de-emphasized, combined, offset or otherwise manipulated to change the probability that it will be received either favourably or unfavourably.

3.45   Important methods to ensure balance include:

- Selection of presentation formats that are not likely to unduly or inappropriately influence assessments made on the basis of the integrated report

- Giving equal consideration to both increases and decreases in the capitals, both strengths and weaknesses of the organization, both positive and negative performance, etc.

- Reporting against previously reported targets, forecasts, projections and expectations.

Freedom from material error

3.46   Freedom from material error does not imply that the information is perfectly accurate in all respects. It does imply that:

- Processes and controls have been applied to reduce to an acceptably low level the risk that reported information contains a material misstatement

- When information includes estimates, this is clearly communicated, and the nature and limitations of the estimation process are explained.

Completeness

3.47   A complete integrated report includes all material information, both positive and negative. To help ensure that all material information has been identified, consideration is given to what organizations in the same industry are reporting on because certain matters within an industry are likely to be material to all organizations in that industry.

3.48   Determining completeness includes considering the extent of information disclosed and its level of specificity or preciseness. This might involve considering potential concerns regarding cost/benefit, competitive advantage and future-oriented information, each of which is discussed below.

Cost/benefit

3.49   Information included in an integrated report is, by nature, central to managing the business. Accordingly, if a matter is important to managing the business, cost should not be a factor in failing to obtain critical information to appropriately assess and manage the matter.

3.50   An organization may evaluate cost and benefits when determining the extent, level of specificity, and preciseness of information necessary for an integrated report to meet its primary purpose, but may not refrain entirely from making any disclosure about a material matter on the basis of cost.

Competitive advantage

3.51 In including information about material matters dealing with competitive advantage (e.g. critical strategies), an organization considers how to describe the essence of the matter without identifying specific information that might cause a significant loss of competitive advantage. Accordingly, the organization considers what advantage a competitor could actually gain from information in an integrated report, and balances this against the need for the integrated report to achieve its primary purpose as noted in paragraph 1.7.

Future-oriented information

3.52 Legal or regulatory requirements may apply to certain future-oriented information in some jurisdictions, covering for example:

- The types of disclosures that may be made

- Whether cautionary statements may be required or permitted to highlight uncertainty regarding achievability

- An obligation to publicly update such information.

3.53 Future-oriented information is by nature more uncertain than historical information. Uncertainty is not, however, a reason in itself to exclude such information. (See also paragraph 5.2 regarding disclosures about uncertainty.)

3G Consistency and comparability

3.54 *The information in an integrated report should be presented:*

- *On a basis that is consistent over time*

- *In a way that enables comparison with other organizations to the extent it is material to the organization's own ability to create value over time.*

Consistency

3.55 Reporting policies are followed consistently from one period to the next unless a change is needed to improve the quality of information reported. This includes reporting the same key performance indicators if they continue to be material across reporting periods. When a significant change has been made, the organization explains the reason for the change, describing (and quantifying if practicable and material) its effect.

Comparability

3.56 The specific information in an integrated report will, necessarily, vary from one organization to another because each organization creates value in its own unique way. Nonetheless, addressing the questions relating to the Content Elements, which apply to all organizations, helps ensure a suitable level of comparability between organizations.

3.57 Other powerful tools for enhancing comparability (in both an integrated report itself and any detailed information that it links to) can include:

- Using benchmark data, such as industry or regional benchmarks

- Presenting information in the form of ratios (e.g. research expenditure as a percentage of sales, or carbon intensity measures such as emissions per unit of output)

- Reporting quantitative indicators commonly used by other organizations with similar activities, particularly when standardized definitions are stipulated by an independent organization (e.g. an industry body). Such indicators are not, however, included in an integrated report unless they are relevant to the individual circumstances of, and are used internally by, the organization.

4. Content Elements

4.1 An integrated report includes eight Content Elements, posed in the form of questions to be answered.

In doing so, it takes into account the general reporting guidance in Chapter 5.

A Organizational overview and external environment

B Governance

C Business model

D Risks and opportunities

E Strategy and resource allocation

F Performance

G Outlook

H Basis of preparation and presentation

4.2 The Content Elements are fundamentally linked to each other and are not mutually exclusive. The order of the Content Elements as listed here is not the only way they could be sequenced; accordingly, the Content Elements are not intended to serve as a standard structure for an integrated report with information about them appearing in a set sequence or as isolated, standalone sections. Rather, information in an integrated report is presented in a way that makes the connections between the Content Elements apparent. (See Section 3B.)

4.3 The content of an organization's integrated report will depend on the individual circumstances of the organization. The Content Elements are therefore stated in the form of questions rather than as checklists of specific disclosures. Accordingly, judgement needs to be exercised in applying the Guiding Principles to determine what information is reported, as well as how it is reported, as discussed below.

4A Organizational overview and external environment

4.4 **An integrated report should answer the question: What does the organization do and what are the circumstances under which it operates?**

4.5 An integrated report identifies the organization's purpose, mission and vision, and provides essential context by identifying matters such as:

- The organization's:
  - Culture, ethics and values
  - Ownership and operating structure
  - Principal activities and markets
  - Competitive landscape and market positioning (considering factors such as the threat of new competition and substitute products or services, the bargaining power of customers and suppliers, and the intensity of competitive rivalry)
  - Position within the value chain.
- Key quantitative information (e.g. the number of employees, revenue and number of countries in which the organization operates), highlighting, in particular, significant changes from prior periods
- Significant factors affecting the external environment and the organization's response.

External environment

4.6 Significant factors affecting the external environment include aspects of the legal, commercial, social, environmental and political context that affect the organization's ability to create value in the short, medium or long term. They can affect the organization directly or indirectly (e.g. by influencing the availability, quality and affordability of a capital that the organization uses or affects).

4.7 These factors occur in the context of the particular organization, in the context of its industry or region, and in the wider social or planetary context. They may include, for example:

- The legitimate needs and interests of key stakeholders
- Macro and micro economic conditions, such as economic stability, globalization, and industry trends
- Market forces, such as the relative strengths and weaknesses of competitors and customer demand
- The speed and effect of technological change
- Societal issues, such as population and demographic changes, human rights, health, poverty, collective values and educational systems

* Environmental challenges, such as climate change, the loss of ecosystems, and resource shortages as planetary limits are approached
* The legislative and regulatory environment in which the organization operates
* The political environment in countries where the organization operates and other countries that may affect the ability of the organization to implement its strategy.

4B   Governance

4.8   *An integrated report should answer the question: How does the organization's governance structure support its ability to create value in the short, medium and long term?*

4.9   An integrated report provides insight about how such matters as the following are linked to its ability to create value:

* The organization's leadership structure, including the skills and diversity (e.g. range of backgrounds, gender, competence and experience) of those charged with governance and whether regulatory requirements influence the design of the governance structure

* Specific processes used to make strategic decisions and to establish and monitor the culture of the organization, including its attitude to risk and mechanisms for addressing integrity and ethical issues

* Particular actions those charged with governance have taken to influence and monitor the strategic direction of the organization and its approach to risk management

* How the organization's culture, ethics and values are reflected in its use of and effects on the capitals, including its relationships with key stakeholders

* Whether the organization is implementing governance practices that exceed legal requirements

* The responsibility those charged with governance take for promoting and enabling innovation

* How remuneration and incentives are linked to value creation in the short, medium and long term, including how they are linked to the organization's use of and effects on the capitals.

4C   Business model

4.10   *An integrated report should answer the question: What is the organization's business model?*

4.11   An organization's business model is its system of transforming inputs, through its business activities, into outputs and outcomes that aims to fulfil the organization's strategic purposes and create value over the short, medium and long term.

4.12   An integrated report describes the business model, including key:

* Inputs (see paragraphs **4.14–4.15**)
* Business activities (see paragraphs 4.16–4.17)
* Outputs (see paragraph 4.18)
* Outcomes (see paragraphs 4.19–4.20).

4.13   Features that can enhance the effectiveness and readability of the description of the business model include:

* Explicit identification of the key elements of the business model

* A simple diagram highlighting key elements, supported by a clear explanation of the relevance of those elements to the organization

* Narrative flow that is logical given the particular circumstances of the organization

* Identification of critical stakeholder and other (e.g. raw material) dependencies and important factors affecting the external environment

* Connection to information covered by other Content Elements, such as strategy, risks and opportunities, and performance (including key performance indicators and financial considerations, such as cost containment and revenues).

Inputs

4.14   An integrated report shows how key inputs relate to the capitals on which the organization depends, or that provide a source of differentiation for the organization, to the extent they are material to understanding the robustness and resilience of the business model.

4.15   An integrated report does not attempt to provide an exhaustive list of all inputs. Rather, the focus is on those that have a material bearing on the ability to create value in the short, medium and long term, whether or not the capitals from which they are derived are owned by the organization. It may also include a discussion of the nature and magnitude of the significant trade-offs that influence the selection of inputs. (See paragraph 5.8.)

Business activities

4.16 An integrated report describes key business activities. This can include:

- How the organization differentiates itself in the market place (e.g. through product differentiation, market segmentation, delivery channels and marketing)

- The extent to which the business model relies on revenue generation after the initial point of sale (e.g. extended warranty arrangements or network usage charges)

- How the organization approaches the need to innovate

- How the business model has been designed to adapt to change.

4.17 When material, an integrated report discusses the contribution made to the organization's long-term success by initiatives such as process improvement, employee training and relationships management.

Outputs

4.18 An integrated report identifies an organization's key products and services. There might be other outputs, such as by-products and waste (including emissions), that need to be discussed within the business model disclosure depending on their materiality.

Outcomes

4.19 An integrated report describes key outcomes. Outcomes are the internal and external consequences (positive and negative) for the capitals as a result of an organization's business activities and outputs. The description of outcomes includes:

- Both internal outcomes (e.g. employee morale, organizational reputation, revenue and cash flows) and external outcomes (e.g. customer satisfaction, tax payments, brand loyalty, and social and environmental effects)

- Both positive outcomes (i.e. those that result in a net increase in the capitals and thereby create value) and negative outcomes (i.e. those that result in a net decrease in the capitals and thereby erode value).

A simple example illustrates the distinction between outputs and outcomes, and the importance of a balanced consideration of outcomes.

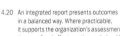

An automotive manufacturer produces internal combustion engine cars as its core output. Positive outcomes include increases in financial capital (through profits to the company and supply chain partners, shareholder dividends and local tax contributions) and enhanced social and relationship capital (through improved brand and reputation, underpinned by satisfied customers and a commitment to quality and innovation).

Negative outcomes include adverse consequences for natural capital (through product-related fossil fuel depletion and air quality reduction) and reduced social and relationship capital (through the influence of product-related health and environmental concerns on social licence to operate).

4.20 An integrated report presents outcomes in a balanced way. Where practicable, it supports the organization's assessment of the use of and effects on the capitals with qualitative and quantitative information. (See paragraphs 1.11, 3.44-3.45, 5.6-5.7.)

4.21 Identifying and describing outcomes, particularly external outcomes, requires an organization to consider the capitals more broadly than those that are owned or controlled by the organization. For example, it may require disclosure of the effects on capitals up and down the value chain (e.g. carbon emissions caused by products the organization manufactures and labour practices of key suppliers). (See also paragraphs 3.30-3.35 regarding determination of the reporting boundary.)

4.22 Some organizations employ more than one business model (e.g. when operating in different market segments). Disaggregating the organization into its material constituent operations and associated business models is important to an effective explanation of how the organization operates.

This requires a distinct consideration of each material business model as well as commentary on the extent of connectivity between the business models (such as the existence of synergistic benefits) unless the organization is run as an investment management business (in which case, it may be appropriate to focus on the investment management business model, rather than the business models of individual investments).

4.23 The integrated report of an organization with multiple businesses often needs to balance disclosure with the need to reduce complexity; however, material information should not be omitted. Aligning external reporting with internal reporting by considering the top level of information that is regularly reported to those charged with governance is ordinarily appropriate.

4D Risks and opportunities

4.24 An integrated report should answer the question: What are the specific risks and opportunities that affect the organization's ability to create value over the short, medium and long term, and how is the organization dealing with them?

4.25 An integrated report identifies the key risks and opportunities that are specific to the organization, including those that relate to the organization's effects on, and the continued availability, quality and affordability of, relevant capitals in the short, medium and long term.

4.26 This can include identifying:

- The specific source of risks and opportunities, which can be internal, external or, commonly, a mix of the two. External sources include those stemming from the external environment, as discussed in paragraphs 4.6–4.7. Internal sources include those stemming from the organization's business activities, as discussed in paragraphs 4.16–4.17.

- The organization's assessment of the likelihood that the risk or opportunity will come to fruition and the magnitude of its effect if it does. This includes consideration of the specific circumstances that would cause the risk or opportunity to come to fruition. Such disclosure will invariably involve a degree of uncertainty. (See also paragraph 5.2 regarding disclosures about uncertainty.)

- The specific steps being taken to mitigate or manage key risks or to create value from key opportunities, including the identification of the associated strategic objectives, strategies, policies, targets and key performance indicators.

4.27 Considering the Guiding Principle materiality, the organization's approach to any real risks (whether they be in the short, medium or long term) that are fundamental to the ongoing ability of the organization to create value and that could have extreme consequences is ordinarily included in an integrated report, even when the probability of their occurrence might be considered quite small.

4E Strategy and resource allocation

4.28 An integrated report should answer the question: Where does the organization want to go and how does it intend to get there?

4.29 An integrated report ordinarily identifies:

- The organization's short-, medium- and long-term strategic objectives

- The strategies it has in place, or intends to implement, to achieve those strategic objectives

- The resource allocation plans it has to implement its strategy

- How it will measure achievements and target outcomes for the short, medium and long term.

4.30 This can include describing:

- The linkage between the organization's strategy and resource allocation plans, and the information covered by other Content Elements, including how its strategy and resource allocation plans:

  - Relate to the organization's business model, and what changes to that business model might be necessary to implement chosen strategies to provide an understanding of the organization's ability to adapt to change

  - Are influenced by/respond to the external environment and the identified risks and opportunities

  - Affect the capitals, and the risk management arrangements related to those capitals.

- What differentiates the organization to give it competitive advantage and enable it to create value, such as:

  - The role of innovation

  - How the organization develops and exploits intellectual capital

  - The extent to which environmental and social considerations have been embedded into the organization's strategy to give it a competitive advantage

  - Key features and findings of stakeholder engagement that were used in formulating its strategy and resource allocation plans.

4F Performance

4.31 An integrated report should answer the question: To what extent has the organization achieved its strategic objectives for the period and what are its outcomes in terms of effects on the capitals?

4.32 An integrated report contains qualitative and quantitative information about performance that may include matters such as:

- Quantitative indicators with respect to targets, risks and opportunities, explaining their significance, their implications, and the methods and assumptions used in compiling them

- The organization's effects (both positive and negative) on the capitals, including material effects on capitals up and down the value chain

- The state of key stakeholder relationships and how the organization has responded to key stakeholders' legitimate needs and interests
- The linkages between past and current performance, and between current performance and the organization's outlook.

4.33 Key performance indicators that combine financial measures with other components (e.g. the ratio of greenhouse gas emissions to sales) or narrative that explains the financial implications of significant effects on other capitals and other causal relationships (e.g. expected revenue growth resulting from efforts to enhance human capital) may be used to demonstrate the connectivity of financial performance with performance regarding other capitals. In some cases, this may also include monetizing certain effects on the capitals (e.g. carbon emissions and water use).

4.34 It may be relevant for the discussion of performance to include instances where regulations have a significant effect on performance (e.g. a constraint on revenues as a result of regulatory rate setting) or the organization's non-compliance with laws or regulations may significantly affect its operations.

4G Outlook

4.35 An integrated report should answer the question: What challenges and uncertainties is the organization likely to encounter in pursuing its strategy, and what are the potential implications for its business model and future performance?

4.36 An integrated report ordinarily highlights anticipated changes over time and provides information, built on sound and transparent analysis, about:

- The organization's expectations about the external environment the organization is likely to face in the short, medium and long term

- How that will affect the organization
- How the organization is currently equipped to respond to the critical challenges and uncertainties that are likely to arise.

4.37 Care is needed to ensure the organization's stated expectations, aspirations and intentions are grounded in reality. They need to be commensurate with the ability of the organization to deliver on the opportunities available to it (including the availability, quality and affordability of appropriate capitals), and a realistic appraisal of the organization's competitive landscape and market positioning, and the risks it faces.

4.38 The discussion of the potential implications, including implications for future financial performance, ordinarily includes discussion of:

- The external environment, and risks and opportunities, with an analysis of how these could affect the achievement of strategic objectives
- The availability, quality and affordability of capitals the organization uses or affects (e.g. the continued availability of skilled labour or natural resources), including how key relationships are managed and why they are important to the organization's ability to create value over time.

4.39 An integrated report may also provide lead indicators, key performance indicators or objectives, relevant information from recognized external sources, and sensitivity analyses. If forecasts or projections are included in reporting the organization's outlook, a summary of related assumptions is useful. Comparisons of actual performance to previously identified targets further enables evaluation of the current outlook.

4.40 Disclosures about an organization's outlook in an integrated report are made taking into account the legal or regulatory requirements to which the organization is subject.

4H Basis of preparation and presentation

4.41 An integrated report should answer the question: How does the organization determine what matters to include in the integrated report and how are such matters quantified or evaluated?

4.42 An integrated report describes its basis of preparation and presentation, including:

- A summary of the organization's materiality determination process (see paragraph **4.43**)
- A description of the reporting boundary and how it has been determined (see paragraphs **4.44–4.47**)
- A summary of the significant frameworks and methods used to quantify or evaluate material matters (see paragraphs 4.48–4.49).

Summary of materiality determination process

4.43 An integrated report includes a summary of the organization's materiality determination process and key judgements. (See paragraphs 3.18–3.20.) This may include:

- Brief description of the process used to identify relevant matters, evaluate their importance and narrow them down to material matters
- Identification of the role of those charged with governance and key personnel in the identification and prioritization of material matters

A link to where a more detailed description of the materiality determination process can be found may also be included.

Reporting boundary

4.44 An integrated report identifies its reporting boundary and explains how it has been determined. (See paragraphs 3.30–3.35.)

4.45 Material risks, opportunities and outcomes attributable to or associated with entities that are included in the financial reporting entity, are reported on in the organization's integrated report.

4.46 Risks, opportunities and outcomes attributable to or associated with other entities/stakeholders are reported on in an integrated report to the extent they materially affect the ability of the financial reporting entity to create value.

4.47 Practical issues might limit the nature and extent of information that can be presented in an integrated report. For example:

- The availability of reliable data with respect to entities the financial reporting entity does not control

- The inherent inability to identify all risks, opportunities and outcomes that will materially affect the ability of the financial reporting entity to create value, particularly in the long term.

It may be appropriate to disclose such limitations, and actions being taken to overcome them, in an integrated report.

Summary of significant frameworks and methods

4.48 An integrated report includes a summary of the significant frameworks and methods used to quantify or evaluate material matters included in the report (e.g. the applicable financial reporting standards used for compiling financial information, a company-defined formula for measuring customer satisfaction, or an industry-based framework for evaluating risks). More detailed explanations might be provided in other communications.

4.49 As noted in paragraph 1.10, when information in an integrated report is similar to or based on other information published by the organization, it is prepared on the same basis as, or is easily reconcilable with, that other information. For example, when a key performance indicator covers a similar topic to, or is based on information published in the organization's financial statements or sustainability report, it is prepared on the same basis, and for the same period, as that other information.

---

5. General Reporting Guidance

5.1 The following general reporting matters are relevant to various Content Elements:

- Disclosure of material matters (see paragraphs 5.2-5.5)
- Disclosures about the capitals (see paragraphs 5.6-5.8)
- Time frames for short, medium and long term (see paragraphs 5.9-5.11)
- Aggregation and disaggregation (see paragraphs 5.12-5.14).

Disclosure of material matters

5.2 Taking the nature of a material matter into consideration, the organization considers providing:

- Key information, such as:
  - An explanation of the matter and its effect on the organization's strategy, business model or the capitals
  - Relevant interactions and interdependencies providing an understanding of causes and effects
  - The organization's view on the matter
  - Actions to manage the matter and how effective they have been
  - The extent of the organization's control over the matter
  - Quantitative and qualitative disclosures, including comparative information for prior periods and targets for future periods.

- If there is uncertainty surrounding a matter, disclosures about the uncertainty, such as:
  - An explanation of the uncertainty
  - The range of possible outcomes, associated assumptions, and how the information could change if the assumptions do not occur as described
  - The volatility, certainty range or confidence interval associated with the information provided.

- If key information about the matter is considered indeterminable, disclosure of that fact and the reason for it

- If significant loss of competitive advantage would result, disclosures of a general nature about the matter, rather than specific details (see paragraph 3.51).

5.3 Depending on the nature of a matter, it may be appropriate to present it on its own in the integrated report or throughout in conjunction with different Content Elements.

5.4 Care is needed to avoid generic disclosures. Information is only included when it is of practical use in achieving the primary purpose of an integrated report as noted in paragraph 1.7. This requires that disclosures be specific to the circumstances of the organization. Accordingly, the bulleted lists of examples and considerations with respect to each Content Element are not meant to be checklists of disclosures, nor is Figure 2 intended to be a fixed template for disclosure purposes. It is important that disclosures are specific to the circumstances of the organization.

Characteristics of quantitative indicators

5.5 Quantitative indicators, such as key performance indicators, can help increase comparability and are particularly helpful in expressing and reporting against targets. Common characteristics of suitable quantitative indicators may include that they are:

- Relevant to the circumstances of the organization

- Consistent with indicators used internally by those charged with governance

- Connected (e.g. they display connectivity between financial and other information)

- Focused on the matters identified by the organization's materiality determination process

- Presented with the corresponding targets, forecasts or projections for two or more future periods

- Presented for multiple periods (e.g. three or more periods) to provide an appreciation of trends

- Presented against previously reported targets, forecasts or projections for the purpose of accountability

- Consistent with generally accepted industry or regional benchmarks to provide a basis for comparison

- Reported consistently over successive periods, regardless of whether the resulting trends and comparisons are favourable or unfavourable.

- Presented with qualitative information to provide context and improve meaningfulness. Relevant qualitative information includes an explanation of:
  - Measurement methods and underlying assumptions
  - The reasons for significant variations from targets, trends or benchmarks, and why they are or are not expected to reoccur.

Disclosures about the capitals

5.6 Disclosures about the capitals, or a component of a capital:

- Are determined by their effects on the organization's ability to create value over time, rather than whether or not they are owned by the organization

- Include the factors that affect their availability, quality and affordability and the organization's expectations of its ability to produce flows from them to meet future demand. This is particularly relevant with respect to capitals that are in limited supply, are non-renewable, and can affect the long-term viability of an organization's business model.

5.7 When it is not practicable or meaningful to quantify significant movements in the capitals, qualitative disclosures are made to explain changes in the availability, quality or affordability of capitals as business inputs and how the organization increases, decreases or transforms them. It is not, however, necessary to quantify or describe the movements between each of the capitals for every matter disclosed.

Complexity, interdependencies and trade-offs

5.8 The <IR> Framework does not require an integrated report to provide an exhaustive account of all the complex interdependencies between the capitals such that an organization's net impact on the global stock of capitals could be tallied. It is important, however, that an integrated report disclose the interdependencies that are considered in determining its reporting boundary, and the important trade-offs that influence value creation over time, including trade-offs:

- Between capitals or between components of a capital (e.g. creating employment through an activity that negatively affects the environment)

- Over time (e.g. choosing one course of action when another course would result in superior capital increment but not until a later period)

- Between capitals owned by the organization and those owned by others or not at all.

Time frames for short, medium and long term

5.9   The future time dimension to be considered in preparing and presenting an integrated report will typically be longer than for some other forms of reporting. The length of each time frame for short, medium and long term is decided by the organization with reference to its business and investment cycles, its strategies, and its key stakeholders' legitimate needs and interests. Accordingly, there is no set answer for establishing the length for each term.

5.10 Time frames differ by:

- Industry or sector (e.g. strategic objectives in the automobile industry typically cover two model-cycle terms, spanning between eight and ten years, whereas within the technology industry, time frames might be significantly shorter)

- The nature of outcomes (e.g. some issues affecting natural or social and relationship capitals can be very long term in nature).

5.11 The length of each reporting time frame and the reason for such length might affect the nature of information disclosed in an integrated report. For example, because longer-term matters are more likely to be more affected by uncertainty, information about them may be more likely to be qualitative in nature, whereas information about shorter-term matters may be better suited to quantification, or even monetization. However, it is not necessary to disclose the effects of a matter for each time frame.

Aggregation and disaggregation

5.12 Each organization determines the level of aggregation (e.g. by country, subsidiary, division, or site) at which to present information that is appropriate to its circumstances. This includes balancing the effort required to disaggregate (or aggregate) information against any added meaningfulness of information reported on a disaggregated (or aggregated) basis.

5.13 In some circumstances, aggregation of information can result in a significant loss of meaning and can also fail to highlight particularly strong or poor performance in specific areas. On the other hand, unnecessary disaggregation can result in clutter that adversely affects the ease of understanding the information.

5.14 The organization disaggregates (or aggregates) information to an appropriate level considering, in particular, how senior management and those charged with governance manage and oversee the organization and its operations. This commonly results in presenting information based on the business or geographical segments used for financial reporting purposes. (See also paragraphs 4.22–4.23 regarding organizations with multiple business models.)

GLOSSARY

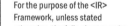

For the purpose of the <IR> Framework, unless stated otherwise, the following terms have the meanings attributed below:

Business model. An organization's system of transforming inputs through its business activities into outputs and outcomes that aims to fulfil the organization's strategic purposes and create value over the short, medium and long term.

Capitals. Stocks of value on which all organizations depend for their success as inputs to their business model, and which are increased, decreased or transformed through the organization's business activities and outputs. The capitals are categorized in the <IR> Framework as financial, manufactured, intellectual, human, social and relationship, and natural.

Content Elements. The categories of information required to be included in an integrated report; the Content Elements, which are fundamentally linked to each other and are not mutually exclusive, are stated in the form of questions to be answered in a way that makes the relationships between them apparent.

Guiding Principles. The principles that underpin the preparation and presentation of an integrated report, informing the content of the report and how information is presented.

Inputs. The capitals (resources and relationships) that the organization draws upon for its business activities.

Integrated report. A concise communication about how an organization's strategy, governance, performance and prospects, in the context of its external environment, lead to the creation, preservation or erosion of value in the short, medium and long term.

Integrated reporting. A process founded on integrated thinking that results in a periodic integrated report by an organization about value creation, preservation or erosion over time and related communications regarding aspects of value creation, preservation or erosion.

Integrated thinking. The active consideration by an organization of the relationships between its various operating and functional units and the capitals that the organization uses or affects. Integrated thinking leads to integrated decision-making and actions that consider the creation, preservation or erosion of value over the short, medium and long term.

Material/materiality. A matter is material if it could substantively affect the organization's ability to create value in the short, medium or long term.

Outcomes. The internal and external consequences (positive and negative) for the capitals as a result of an organization's business activities and outputs.

Outputs. An organization's products and services, and any by-products and waste.

Performance. An organization's achievements relative to its strategic objectives, and its outcomes in terms of its effects on the capitals.

Providers of financial capital. Equity and debt holders and others who provide financial capital, both existing and potential, including lenders and other creditors. This includes the ultimate beneficiaries of investments, collective asset owners, and asset or fund managers.

Reporting boundary. The boundary within which matters are considered relevant for inclusion in an organization's integrated report.

Stakeholders. Those groups or individuals that can reasonably be expected to be significantly affected by an organization's business activities, outputs or outcomes, or whose actions can reasonably be expected to significantly affect the ability of the organization to create value over time. Stakeholders may include providers of financial capital, employees, customers, suppliers, business partners, local communities, NGOs, environmental groups, legislators, regulators and policy-makers.

Strategy. Strategic objectives together with the strategies to achieve them.

Those charged with governance. The person(s) or organization(s) (e.g. the board of directors or a corporate trustee) with responsibility for overseeing the strategic direction of an organization and its obligations with respect to accountability and stewardship. For some organizations and jurisdictions, those charged with governance may include executive management.

Value creation, preservation or erosion. The process that results in increases, decreases or transformations of the capitals caused by the organization's business activities and outputs.

Using the <IR> Framework

Form of report and relationship with other information

1.12 *An integrated report should be a designated, identifiable communication.*

Application of the <IR> Framework

1.17 *Any communication claiming to be an integrated report and referencing the Framework should apply all the requirements identified in bold italic type unless:*

- *The unavailability of reliable information or specific legal prohibitions results in an inability to disclose material information*

- *Disclosure of material information would cause significant competitive harm.*

1.18 *In the case of the unavailability of reliable information or specific legal prohibitions, an integrated report should:*

- *Indicate the nature of the information that has been omitted*

- *Explain the reason why it has been omitted*

- *In the case of the unavailability of data, identify the steps being taken to obtain the information and the expected time frame for doing so.*

Responsibility for an integrated report

1.20 *An integrated report should include a statement from those charged with governance that includes:*

- *An acknowledgement of their responsibility to ensure the integrity of the integrated report*

- *Their opinion or conclusion about whether, or the extent to which, the integrated report is presented in accordance with the <IR> Framework.*

Where legal or regulatory requirements preclude a statement of responsibility from those charged with governance, this should be clearly stated.

GUIDING PRINCIPLES

Strategic focus and future orientation

3.3 *An integrated report should provide insight into the organization's strategy, and how that relates to its ability to create value in the short, medium and long term and to its use of and effects on the capitals.*

Connectivity of information

3.6 *An integrated report should show a holistic picture of the combination, interrelatedness and dependencies between the factors that affect the organization's ability to create value over time.*

Stakeholder relationships

3.10 *An integrated report should provide insight into the nature and quality of the organization's relationships with its key stakeholders, including how and to what extent the organization understands, takes into account and responds to their legitimate needs and interests.*

Materiality

3.17 *An integrated report should disclose information about matters that substantively affect the organization's ability to create value over the short, medium and long term.*

Conciseness

3.36 *An integrated report should be concise.*

Reliability and completeness

3.39 *An integrated report should include all material matters, both positive and negative, in a balanced way and without material error.*

Consistency and comparability

3.54 *The information in an integrated report should be presented:*

- *On a basis that is consistent over time*
- *In a way that enables comparison with other organizations to the extent it is material to the organization's own ability to create value over time.*

CONTENT ELEMENTS

Organizational overview and external environment

4.4 *An integrated report should answer the question: What does the organization do and what are the circumstances under which it operates?*

Governance

4.8 *An integrated report should answer the question: How does the organization's governance structure support its ability to create value in the short, medium and long term?*

Business model

4.10 *An integrated report should answer the question: What is the organization's business model?*

Risks and opportunities

4.24 *An integrated report should answer the question: What are the specific risks and opportunities that affect the organization's ability to create value over the short, medium and long term, and how is the organization dealing with them?*

Strategy and resource allocation

4.28 *An integrated report should answer the question: Where does the organization want to go and how does it intend to get there?*

Performance

4.31 *An integrated report should answer the question: To what extent has the organization achieved its strategic objectives for the period and what are its outcomes in terms of effects on the capitals?*

Outlook

4.35 *An integrated report should answer the question: What challenges and uncertainties is the organization likely to encounter in pursuing its strategy, and what are the potential implications for its business model and future performance?*

Basis of preparation and presentation

4.41 *An integrated report should answer the question: How does the organization determine what matters to include in the integrated report and how are such matters quantified or evaluated?*

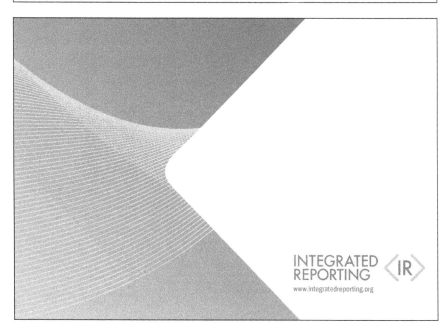

Appendix 2 King IV on a Page

This graphic sets out the principles in *The King IV Report on Corporate Governance for South Africa 2016.*[*] It has been reproduced with the kind permission of the Institute of Directors in South Africa.

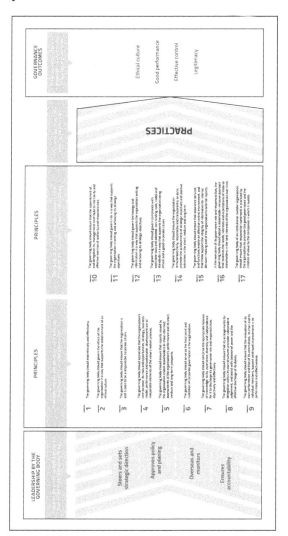

* Copyright and trademarks are owned by the Institute of Directors in South Africa. The IoDSA website is at http://www.iodsa.co.za/?page=AboutKingIV.

Lightning Source UK Ltd.
Milton Keynes UK
UKHW032200170821
389030UK00004B/416